Authentic Memoirs Of Mrs. Clarke

Elizabeth Taylor, Mary Anne Thompson Clarke

MEMOIRS

OF

MRS. CLARKE.

T. Plummer, Printer, Seething Lane.

Engraved by Hopwood, from a drawing, by Erskine.

M.rs Clarke.

Published by Thomas Tegg, III. Cheapside 1809.

AUTHENTIC
MEMOIRS
OF
MRS. CLARKE,

IN WHICH IS POURTRAYED

THE SECRET HISTORY

AND

Intrigues

OF MANY CHARACTERS IN THE

FIRST CIRCLES OF FASHION AND HIGH LIFE;

And containing the whole of

HER CORRESPONDENCE

During the Time she lived under the Protection of

HIS ROYAL HIGHNESS

THE DUKE OF YORK,

The gallant

DUKE'S LOVE LETTERS,

And other interesting

PAPERS NEVER BEFORE PUBLISHED.

———

BY

MISS ELIZABETH TAYLOR.

———

SECOND EDITION.

══════════════════

LONDON:
PRINTED FOR THOMAS TEGG,
No. 111,
OPPOSITE BOW CHURCH, CHEAPSIDE.
1809.

AUTHENTIC

MEMOIRS

OF

MRS. MARY ANN CLARKE.

———

CHASTITY has ever been deemed the most exalted female virtue—the jewel which alone elevated its possessor in the estimation of society, and the absence of which renders woman stigmatized, degraded, and worthless. Every man is willing to subscribe to this in theory: but it is continually opposed by practical contradiction; for we daily find instances of women whose incontinence has been the most glaring and the most disgusting to manly delicacy, commanding the adoration, and constituting the felicity of the most exalted characters. This is a consideration which ought not to be

B

passed over lightly. If chastity be of such inesti-
mable value as that which we attach to it in theory,
let not all the blandishments of fortune, talent,
beauty, and polished manners, give to a worthless object power over our hearts and understandings: on
the other hand, if it be not; if it be of so little consequence in the way of fixing regard, then let not
female frailty, unvarnished by those acquisitions and
accomplishments, degrade the victim of error be-
neath her true rank and level in society. This op-
position between theory and practice ought not to be
passed over without thought. The moment a female
deviates from the path of rectitude, or rather the moment she commits an act of incontinence, she is called worthless, and often infamous; but look at the
conduct of those men, who are continually in the
habit of throwing these censures, and what sort of a
picture does it offer to our contemplation? Whilst
frigid unalluring chastity—cold conjugal fidelity, sits
moping in neglect and solitude, unable to fix the
faithless wanderer, the fascinating prostitute waves
her wand like a sorceress, draws him within the ma-
gic circle of pleasure; and moral duty, domestic

affection, with every tie that cements society, is swallowed up in sensual indulgence.

" The web of our life is of a mingled yarn." There is no character so vicious as not to possess some portion of virtue; nor, on the other hand, is there any virtue but what is sufficiently tempered with human imperfection. The woman of untainted character will often be found infected with pride and envy, sometimes prone to detraction, without feeling for misfortune, or mercy for human frailty; while on the other hand, the courtesan may often be found possessing a heart replete with the milk of human kindness, and " a hand, open as the day to melting charity." These considerations candour demands of us in entering upon an undertaking like the present; but though, whilst contemplating the character of her who forms the subject of these memoirs, we would make every fair allowance for those failings which are but too conspicuous in her character, we must give the cause of morality fair play; we must observe that the reign of vice appears to be short and uncertain, affording

no pleasure in retrospect, leaving nothing behind
which can serve as a prop to the mind in the hour
of calamity, while, on the contrary, virtuous self-
denial, gives a true relish of life; and will, at every
period of existence, prove a source of cheering reflection. Woman comes from the hand of her
Maker impressed with a delicacy of feeling, which,
when once obliterated, the charm is gone which regulated the whole moral character. When the
bonds of early affection have been broken, no attachment is found in which the heart has any con-
cern. Pleasure and parade are the only objects of
pursuit—Life is passed in satiety, and terminated
in languor, disappointment, and disgust.

Amidst times of most portentous aspect, when
political topics of the utmost importance to the
cause of Europe agitated the public mind, and fixed
general attention, a female of obscure origin starts
all at once into notoriety, and the fate of armies,
the disasters of war, and the downfal of kingdoms,
are all put to flight by the interest which she ex-
cites. Her character and conduct are the theme of

every tongue, and every circumstance of her life is enquired into with the most eager curiosity: We have no intention in the course of the present work to enter into a discussion of those important questions relative to the alledged existence of dangerous abuses in the military department of the state, that have formed the basis of that enquiry which called our heroine into notice—these have been so amply sifted and discussed by members of parliament and the prints of the day, that for any single individual to pronounce an opinion upon the guilt or innocence of the illustrious personage who has been the object of the enquiry, would be, in some degree, an insult to the understanding of a British public. This is a subject upon which every one will think and decide for himself. If his Royal Highness the Duke of York be guilty, of what has been urged against him, all the efforts of legal ingenuity exerted and combined in his favour will only enlarge the features of moral turpitude, and render them more odious and disgusting. On the contrary, if he be really innocent, if he be as his friends would represent him, no more than the victim of popular clamour, that

B 3

popular clamour, like the idle blast, will soon pass by, and history will do justice to his character. Neither is it our intention to bring the character of the Royal Duke to the bar of religion and virtue. Rigid morality is more to be wished for than expected in this age of luxury and dissipation, and were every man to be publicly exposed, who sometimes deserts his home to revel in the arms of a mistress, the Duke might say to many of his accusers, " Let him that is without sin amongst you cast the first stone."

The connection of His Royal Highness with Mrs. Clarke has been stigmatised as a double adultery; but this is in our opinion straining morality too far. There are none of the odious and detestable features of that too fashionable vice to be discovered in the connection we are speaking of; he entered not the mansion of domestic felicity and employed seductive arts to alienate the affections of a faithful wife; he found her separated from a husband whom she seems to have formed a determination never to cohabit with again; it is true, by the laws of the country, she was bound to another man, but what human laws can fetter the will of a woman? His Royal Highness found Mrs. Clarke literally " *a loose fish*," an enterprising adventuress in the field of gallantry, consequently as fair an object of his attention as that of any other individual. With respect to the other branch of this double adultery, as it has been uncharitably named, such adultery, it is to be feared, is so common in the higher walks of society, that it can hardly be expected to startle the conscience of a Royal Duke!

The heroine of these pages neither derived her existence from parents distinguished either for wealth or genius, nor was the place of her birth and early residence the best calculated to inculcate those moral virtues which constitute the brightest jewels of the female character.

Her father's name was Thompson, who resided in Bowl and Pin Alley, near White's Alley, Chancery Lane, where Miss Thompson was ushered into the world, as Sterne says, with "squalls of disapprobation at the journey she was compelled to perform."

In this neighbourhood, the moral atmosphere of which was contaminated by the vices of some of the most abandoned prostitutes upon the *pavee*, Miss Thompson, who was naturally of a sprightly and fascinating character, soon attracted the notice of every passing stranger, and, like the lilly of the desert, exhibited her graces to the greater advantage in proportion as they were contrasted with the obscurity of her situation.

Upon the death of her father, the mother of Miss Thompson entered upon a second matrimonial connection with a Mr. Farquhar, who worked as a compositor in the printing-house of Mr. Hughes.

Miss Thompson, whose sprightlier faculties were at an early period in a state of mutiny with the slow-paced drudgery of the needle, now first acquired the rudiments of that knowledge, which, if it did not lead her to distinguish herself in the literary world, and rival in fame the Sewards, the Mores, or the Cowleys, at least enabled her to move more appropriately in that station to which she was subsequently elevated.

Through the influence of her father-in-law, Miss Thompson obtained occasionally employment in reading copy to the person employed as corrector of the press, in which situation she soon attracted the notice of the son of the overseer of the same printing-office, who wishing at the same time to encourage her merit, and to derive pleasure, and, perhaps, future assistance from the cultivation of her talents, placed this young lady, whom he fondly destined as his future wife, at a genteel boarding-school, at Ham, in the county of Essex.

In this, however, as it too frequently happens when the heart and the head cease to in unison, Mr. Day was mistaken. The young lady, whose capacity for elegant improvements was of the very first class, and which could only be equalled by the rapidity with which she acquired them, after remaining two years at school, returned home, it is said, with ideas very much altered from those which her benefactor had wished to have inspired.

Whether from the conscious superiority of her charms, or from the proud attainments she had acquired, or perhaps from an union of both, her conduct towards her admirer became very much altered. Alarmed at this unexpected change, Mr. Day frequently remonstrated, but his remonstrances were as frequently retorted with contradiction or disdain.

With true lovers, indeed, quarrels are almost proverbial, and tend more firmly to cement the union of hearts,

> In amore hæc omnia sunt inimicitiæ.
> Bellum Pax rursum.

But in these bickerings

> Love was not in their looks,
> Neither to God——nor to each other.

Whether or not the " crown and hearted throne of Love was yielded up to tyrannous hate," or lessened by the young lady's disdain, or the affection of Mr.

Day subsided into the tranquillity of indifference, is not material here to examine; certain it is, that these frequent bickerings ultimately terminated in an open rupture.

About this period Mr. and Mrs. Farquhar removed from Bowl and Pin Alley to Black Raven Passage, Cursitor Street, Holborn.

Miss Thompson was now about sixteen, a period when female charms are in full blossom; the graces of her person were improved by cultivation—warm, easy, affable, she charmed wherever she moved, her address rivetted the fetters which her eyes had forged; nor was even age itself proof against her fascination.

Charms such as her's would stir an holy hermit.

Her fascinating manners and the graces of her person, far out-pace the powers of the pen. One glance of her eye would impress them more strongly than any description, were such description extended to a folio.

Such Helen was, and who can blame the boy,
That in so bright a flame consum'd his Troy?

B 6

nor was it yet that the superb service of plate (such is
the instability of human greatness), which formerly
decorated the luxurious table of a prince of the
blood royal of France, nor was it yet that the jewels
presented to the darling of his heart, by the field-
marshall of Great-Britain, had found their way to
those superior magazines of temporary accommodation, which are appropriately situated at an end of
the town distinguished for the wealth and rank of its
inhabitants; it was neither plate nor jewels, but
wearing apparel, the humbler appendages of obscurity, shifts, petticoats, &c. which first produced the
supplies of necessity, and with these Miss Thompson
was occasionally dispatched for the relief of the
family.

In this line, amongst other persons in the same
accommodating business, Miss Thompson is said to
have attracted the attention of Mr. F——l——d, of
Golden Lane, in whose good opinion our young
financier so effectually insinuated herself, as to dazzle
even his " just judging and instructed eye;" not exactly with respect to the actual value of the articles

offered for pledge, but at least she worked so far
upon his feelings, as to induce him to advance more
than persons of his mercenary cast are usually in the
habit of lending.

To him, therefore, her visits became more frequent,
whenever temporary accommodation became necessary; and no higher idea can be formed of the fascinations of our heroine, than that they could charm
the mercenary serpent of avarice, and even, we had
almost said, *the heart* of *a pawnbroker.*

> The ill-bred ruffian and pale usurer,
> If Love's atmosphere such hearts can warm,
> May safely mellow into love, and grow
> Refin'd, humane, and generous, if they can :
> Love in such bosoms never, to a fault,
> Or pain, or pleases.

Although, from the habits of these licensed usurers, their hearts are not likely to be affected by
those finer sensations, those thrilling emotions, which
we find in more elevated situations; and although
the heart of a pawnbroker is not the best calculated for the throne of the all-potent god, yet,

whether actuated by love or lust, Mr. F. nevertheless, certainly did feel, as Strap says, so much of a
"sneaking inclination" towards his young customer,
as to induce him to admit her occasionally into his
private cabinet, a commodious back-parlour, where
it is said the value of the specific articles offered as
pledges did not always constitute the topic of conversation.

Miss Thompson was now scarcely seventeen, when
she changed her situation for a wife. Amongst

"The am'rous youths who found her bow'd,"

was Mr. Joseph Clarke, the second son of a weal-
thy bricklayer, in Angel-court, Snow-hill, but who
now resides at Kettering, in Northamptonshire, with
his younger brother, and his brother's wife, the former of whom was brought up at Cambridge.

Mr. Joseph Clarke was bound apprentice to Mr.
Burnell, the corner of Black Raven-passage, Cursi-
tor-street. He had just emancipated himself from

the fetters of apprenticeship, and had attained that
period

> When youth elate and gay,
> 'Steps into life, and follows unrestrain'd,
> Where passion drives, or prudence points the way.

So persuasive were the arguments of Mr. Clarke
with Miss Thompson, that they soon eloped from
the confined air of an alley, to enjoy the delights
of love in the purer atmosphere of Pentonville, in
which neighbourhood Mrs. Clarke first became a
mother.

About this time the enamoured couple removed
to Charles-square, Hoxton, where they were known
and visited by a very respectable circle of acquaintance.

As Mr. Clarke, who as we have before observed,
had served his apprenticeship to Mr. Burnell, the
stone-mason, was not in business, and he was supported only by the allowance he received from his
father, the supplies not unfrequently fell short, and

the demon of necessity occasionally drove love out of the window; the little god was not, however, completely expelled from the house, for we find the lady becomes a second time

"As women wish to be who love their lords."

And so satisfied was Mr. Clarke of the propriety of the demeanour of his paramour, that, it is said, previous to the birth of his third child, as appears by the register of Pancras-church, he plighted his troth to her at the altar; and thus, when about the age of eighteen, she assumed a legal right to the name under which she now passes.

After a residence of nearly two years in Hoxton-square, Mr. and Mrs. Clarke went to reside in Golden-lane, where, from the liberality of his father, he, Mr. Clarke, was enabled to commence business as a stone-mason.

Here, for a time, every thing went smoothly on, and it might have been supposed, that, with such a

companion so pre-eminently gifted both in mind
and person, her husband could have no temptations for leaving the fair mountain of chaste
delight, to batten on the moor of mercenary pros-
titution; such, however, is human frailty, such
the paroxysms of intemperance and debauchery,
that, from some discoveries not admitting palliation,
Mrs. Clarke formed the resolution of breaking a
connection, which, longer continued, might have
involved in distress or infamy, twice the number of
innocent individuals the family then consisted of,
and made indiscriminately the pledges of love the
victims of the union.

It was in the year 1794, that Mr. Clarke commenced business in Golden-lane, where, (as was
proved by Mr. Stower of Charterhouse-square, who
frequently visited in the family,) he continued about
three or four years.

During this period it was that the parents and
their family were reduced to practise all the expedients of " hard shifting woe;" the extravagance of

the husband, who, from being of a convivial turn, had a large circle of companions of the same propensity, kept the ingenuity of the wife eternally upon the rack to find the necessary supplies.

The parlour of the public-house now became the substitute for the counting-house, and the skittle-ground a more congenial stage of action with Mr. Clarke, than the stone-yard; and in proportion as the public-house and its gambling allurements obtained the ascendency, the counting-house and the stone-yard became irksome.

Business was now neglected, and after all the various expedients usually had recourse to, by declining tradesmen for bolstering up their credit—from the *licenced usury* of the pawnbroker, to the disinterested accommodations of those, who conceive they steer clear of the strict letter of the law, by discounting doubtful paper, at the usual interest, with the trifling addition of *half the money* advanced to be laid out in goods—after running the gauntlet between pawnbrokers, usurers, and attornies, the centre of gravity of Mr. Clarke's credit, which had been gradually declining, at length fell completely beyond the base, and a commission of bankruptcy was sued out against him by Mr. Alderman Staines.

It was during this period that Mrs. Clarke had to contend with difficulties in various shapes; and fiends of distress, in all their terrible forms, infested that bed which had once been the rosy bower of love, and haunted that house, before the mansion of peace and felicity.

It was now, in the continual family committee of supplies and ways and means, that Mrs. Clarke acquired those facilities of resource to stave off the " exigencies of existing circumstances," which would have well qualified her for the office of chancellor of the exchequer, and, by her fascinating powers, the syren soon found means to render the industry and wealth of others subservient to her temporary occasions.

It was whilst labouring under these pecuniary embarrassments that Mrs. Clarke again resorted to the exchequer, in Golden-lane, where she learned that her old acquaintance Mr. F——l——d, (although such a circumstance is not very usual for persons in his line), had become a bankrupt, and she recognised as his successor, the young gentleman who, in his master's prosperity, had acted in the humbler capacity of his shopman.

Whether, however, his heart was less assailable by female fascinations, or that interest was the only magnet that could attract his affections, young *Two-to-one* was not to be bled so freely as his master. " Two upon a horse," they say, " seldom ride well ;" thus, where money constituted the object of both, they soon reciprocally discovered what constituted the magnet of mutual attraction ; and no sooner was this discovery made than the poles became as diametrically repellent as in the more liberal days of Mr. F——l——d, they had been so mutually attractive.

This was certainly the most important period of
Mrs. Clarke's life, the period when she made that
sacrifice of character which can never be retrieved;
a period when her prospects were to assume a new
aspect, and her feelings, her sentiments, her habits,
to experience a total revolution. We wish not to
become the apologists of female depravity; but we
must, nevertheless, in candour allow, that the first
step of Mrs. Clarke from the path of rectitude was
accompanied with no very inferior circumstances of
palliation.

When a man, after all the tender assiduities of
the lover, has succeeded in obtaining the heart and
the person of a beautiful woman, he is too apt to
relax in those delicate attentions which originally
won her heart, and can alone keep alive the flame of
love. There is a species of homage which a woman
like Mrs. Clarke naturally looks for from the other
sex; it is the case, perhaps, with all women; but it
must have been more particularly so with one so
formed to inspire love and command adoration and

respect. We know not what may have been the feelings of her husband when deprived of the treasure he once possessed; and which, till to him for ever lost, perhaps he " prized not to its value." We have, however, no hesitation in pronouncing, that the man who should be so flatteringly distinguished by the preference of a female, so gifted in mind and person as Mrs. Clarke, must necessarily have been a happy man, so long as she maintained the character of a virtuous wife. It is not, perhaps, easy to pronounce, in a case where the silent monitions of conscience can alone decide; but the man who is conscious of having, by his vicious habits, and by a neglect which no woman can well endure, but least of all such a woman as Mrs. Clarke—we must repeat, that the man who is conscious of having driven such a woman from the cool sequestered vale of domestic life, to plunge into an ocean of infamy, can have no very pleasant companion in private reflection. Such a character must, if his feelings be, in any degree correct, carry inseparably, in his bosom a remorse that must make his life truly wretched.

both of his bill and the costs afterwards, upon her removal to Gloucester-Place, upon sending her the following letter and enclosure:—

"Madam,

"As I have not heard from you in reply to my last letter, I think myself justified in informing you, that in the course of a week the inclosed hand-bill will be published, which no doubt will prevent any other tradesman from subjecting himself to similar treatment. As the wording of the bill has received the legal sanction of very able men in the profession, I am perfectly at ease in regard to any additional threats that may be held out to me.

"I remain

"Your obedient servant,

"JOHN FEW, jun."

"22 *June*, 1804.

"Mrs. Clarke, Gloucester-Place,
"No. 18, Portman-square."

" Caution to Tradesmen

" This is to give notice to the tradesmen in the neighbourhood of Portman-square, that they cannot recover by law, any debt from Mrs. Mary Ann Clarke, formerly of Tavistock-Place, Russell-Square, but now of Gloucester-Place, she being a married woman, and her husband now living, though his place of residence was *unknown* even to herself or her mother. These facts were proved on the trial of an action lately brought by a tradesman in Holborn, against this Mrs. Mary Ann Clarke, for goods *actually* sold and delivered to *her*; but she availing herself of her coverture (which, to the great surprise of the plaintiff, she *contrived* to prove,) he could not by law obtain any part of his demand; and being consequently nonsuited, an execution for *her* costs was, by her attorney, *actually* put into his, the tradesman's, house.

This might afford ground to charge our heroine with want of principle; but we think the accusation must fall to the ground upon a candid investigation of the evidence that has transpired upon the

D

late enquiry. The chief point upon which she appears anxious, when deserted by the Duke of York, is to obtain the means of paying her tradesmen's bills.

Indeed, from 1804 to 1806, the period in which she had an establishment in Gloucester-Place, her resources were by no means equal to her scale of expences.

Mrs. Favory says, that after the first quarter, she could never pay her debts properly. People were teazing her to pieces for money, and saying that she kept it. She adds, that when she informed her mistress of these *teazing* applications the answer she received was, that his Royal Highness was very backward in his payments, and that she must put the people off, which she, Mrs. F. accordingly did.

The upholstery, it seems, was furnished by Oakley, in Bond-street; the china and glass by Mortlock, of Oxford-street; the grates by Summers and Rose, Bond-street; and the plate by Birkett.

Besides these, Mrs. Clarke had some dealings with Parker, in Fleet-street, and occasionally with Turner, in Princes-street. Sometimes these gentlemen refused to furnish the articles; and were clamorous to know whether his Royal Highness had *settled with Mrs. Clarke, and given her money.* To which Mrs. Favory would reply in the negative, but as soon as she had it, she would give it them.

We cannot better describe the complete subjection of our British Mars to this modern Venus, than by submitting to inspection some of those amatory effusions which would throw the strains of an Ovid or Tibullus, a Petrarch or a Hammond, completely in the back ground.

Many of those tender billets have been indeed destroyed, which shewed how little consequence the deity, to whose shrine this incense of flattering subjection was offered, attached to her worshipper; and how truly the Field-Marshal of Great Britain, the motto of whose private seal was " Never Absent" was in this instance as mistaken as his.

mistress was successful in selecting for her device *Cupid riding on an ass,* with the appropriate motto *Tels sont mes sujets*—" For further particulars enquire within."

———

" *August* 4, 1805."

" How can I sufficiently express to my sweetest my darling love, the delight which her dear, her pretty letter gave me, or how much I feel all the kind things she says to me in it ? Millions and millions of thanks for it, my angel! and be assured that my heart is fully sensible of your affection, and that upon it alone its whole happiness depends.

" I am, however, quite hurt that my love did not go to the Lewes Races; how kind of her to think of me upon the occasion! but I trust that she knows me too well not to be convinced that I cannot bear the idea of adding to those sacrifices which I am but too sensible that she has made to me.

" News my angel cannot expect from me from hence; though the life led here, at least, in the family I am in, is very hurrying, there is a sameness in it which affords little subject for a letter; except Lord Chesterfield's family, there is not a single person except ourselves that I know. Last night we were at the play, which went off better than the first night.

"*Dr. O'Meara called upon me yesterday morning, and delivered me your letter; he wishes much to preach before royalty, and if I can put him in the way of it I will.*

"What a time it appears to me already, my Darling, since we parted; how impatiently I look forward to next Wednesday se'nnight!

"God bless you, my own dear, dear Love! I shall miss the post if I add more? Oh! believe me ever, to my last hour, your's and your's alone."

Addressed:

"Mrs. Clarke,

"to be left at the Post-office, Worthing."

Indorsed:

"Dr. O'Meara."

D 3

" Sandgate, August 24, 1804.

" How can I sufficiently express to my darling Love, my thanks for her dear, dear letter, or the delight which the assurances of her love give me ! Oh ! my angel ! do me justice, and be convinced that there never was a woman adored as you are. Every day, every hour convinces me more and more, that my whole happiness depends upon you alone. What a time it appears to be since we parted, and with what impatience do I look forward to the day after to-morrow ; there are still however two whole nights before I shall clasp my darling in my arms!

" How happy am I to learn that you are better ; I still, however, will not give up my hopes of the cause of your feeling uncomfortable. *Clavering is mistaken, my angel, in thinking that any new regiments are to be raised ; it is not intended, only second battalions to the existing corps ; you had better, therefore, tell him so, and that you were sure that there would be no use in applying for him.*

„Ten thousand thanks, my love, for the hand-kerchiefs, which are delightful; and I need not, I trust, assure you of the pleasure I feel in wearing them, and thinking of the dear hands who made them for me.

" Nothing could be more satisfactory than the tour I have made, and the state in which I have found every thing. The whole of the day before yesterday was employed in visiting the works at Dover; reviewing the troops there, and examining the coast as far as this place. From Folkstone I had a very good view of those of the French camp.

" Yesterday I first reviewed the camp here, and afterwards the 14th Light Dragoons, who are certainly in very fine order: and from thence proceeded to Brabourne Lees, to see four regiments of militia; which, altogether, took me up near thirteen hours. I am now setting off immediately to ride along the coast to Hastings, reviewing the different corps as I pass, which will take me at least as long. Adieu, therefore, my sweetest, dearest love, till the

day after to-morrow, and be assured that to my
last hour I shall ever remain your's and your's
alone.

Addressed :
" George Farquhar, Esq.
" No. 18, Gloucester-Place, Portman-square."
FOLKSTONE,
79, Indorsed :
" Gen. Clavering, &c."

———

Before we proceed with other billet doux from
the Duke, we shall, in pursuance of our plan,
illustrate and explain, by other written documents. stated in the minutes of the House of Commons, not only the ascendency which our heroine
possessed over the mind of her paramour, but the
various modes and departments in which this
agency was exerted.

We wish. however, here to state distinctly, that
we do not mean to enter, except in a very partial
degree, upon the oral examinations at the bar of the
House, but on the contrary by bringing together

and contrasting the written documents, to give as
clear and perspicuous a view of the case as can be
found in any publication upon the subject, without
excepting the minutes of the House of Commons,
which are now before us, and from whence the accuracy of our statement may be relied upon.

To return to the preceding letters—That the
tender passion was not alone the object of the
Royal Duke's correspondence, at least with Mrs.
Clarke is obvious. She contrived occasionally to
intermix some enquiries relative to the traffic she
was carrying on, to which the Duke, although acquitted by a majority of the House, composed,
however, of the usual materials which constitute
ministerial majorities, of any direct connivance or
participation in the bribe, nevertheless must be
admitted not completely to have been *guiltlessly
innocent* ; although, if any term may be allowed
to characterize the tortueus windings and special
pleadings of Mr. Perceval's resolutions, he must
at least be admitted to have been *innocently guilty*
of the charges against him.

In the midst of the Dearies and Darlings, and all the honeyed sentences, we had almost said of love, we find two topics of business, in answer to some applications from the mistress of the Duke, in favour of her protegees; and two characters are brought upon the stage, viz, Doctor O'Meara, who wanted to purchase a Mitre,—

So into God's fold lewd hirelings climb,—

and General Clavering, who wanted a regiment.

We proceed to illustrate the reasons why this Reverend *would-be* Father in God, and this intriguing General were mentioned by the Royal Duke in his letter to his mistress.

Amongst the documents found amongst Mrs. Clarke's papers, was the testimonial of the Archbishop of Tuam, bearing testimony to the most unexceptionable character, independence, &c. It is as follows:

" Sir,

" In consequence of your application to me, I am ready to give ample satisfaction, and to bear testimony, that I have had assurances from persons in whom I place the most implicit confidence, that you are a gentleman of most unexceptionable character in every respect; of a respectable family and independent fortune. I have tht honour to be,

Sir,

Your most obedient humble servant,

W. TUAM."

Crescent, Bath, Feb. 17, 1806.

Addressed:
The Rev. Dr. O'Meara,
  No. 7. Alfred-Street.

⸻

Here we find the credentials of the Rev. Father in God, in the possession of the Duke's mistress. Mrs. Clarke says, " the very night that the Duke was going to Weymouth, the Dr. called upon her, the moment the Duke had left the house at *midnight*;" that she thinks he must have watched the Duke out ! that the Doctor, who came in just as she was upon the stairs, said it was a very good opportunity, for he was going to Weymouth immediately, and asked her to come down stairs again, and write him a letter of introduction, which she did.

This evidence is fully corroborated by the expression in the Duke's letter, viz.

" Doctor O'Meara called upon me yesterday morning, and delivered me your letter; he wishes much to preach before royalty, and if I can put him in the way of it I will."

Mrs. Clarke's Examination.

Did you ever communicate Dr. O'Meara's offer for a bishopric to the Commander in Chief?— Yes, I did, and *all his documents.*

What was the Commander in Chief's answer? That he had preached before his Majesty, and his Majesty did not like the O in his name.

The Duke's letter was dated August 24, 1804. The following *paragraph* appears in the Morning Post, under the head of Weymouth, October 3, 1805, viz

" The Rev. Dr. O'Meara preached on Sunday an excellent Sermon (from Rom. ch. xii. 5.) on Universal Benevolence. He expatiated with great eloquence on the relation which the *public* and *private* affections bears to each other, and their use in the moral system. He inveighed with peculiar energy against the savage philosophy of the *French Deists,* who propose to erect a system of universal philanthrophy upon the ruins of the *private affections* which regard kindred, friends, benefactors, and the poor, thus inverting the eternal order of nature, by violently transferring all the lovely train of social affections from our relatives and friends to distant and unknown myriads. Whilst under these vague terms of attachment to, and of advancing the general good, the practice of every debasing vice finds a shelter, and the perpetration of every horrid crime a subterfuge. We wish our young ecclesiastics would arouse themselves, and shake off that mental langour which oppresses them in the pulpit, and shew themselves *in earnest.* *Sacred eloquence* is certainly in *this country* feeble and unimpressive; no other excellence can supply the want of animation. That sweet charm, that *celestial unction,* which Christian oratory demands, this gentleman possesses in an eminent degree. ' *His lips are touched with the live coal from off the altar.'* The King was very attentive, and stood for nearly the whole of the sermon, (which we never observed before) and *expressed his high approbation to the Earl of Uxbridge and others, whilst the Queen and Princesses, and the whole audience were melted into tears."*

It is true, indeed, that the investigation in the House of Commons was confined to abuses in the army. Nothing, however, can more strongly evince the extensive influence of Mrs. Clarke over every department which papa's favorite boy could influence or control. The allusion in the letter is

we trust, sufficiently explained, and further infe-
rence or comment would be insulting the judgment of our readers.

We now proceed to explain how far " General
Clavering (now upon duty at the Old Bailey) was
mistaken," and although he declared, at the Bar of
the House, he did not conceive that Mrs. Clarke
had any influence with his Royal Highness, we
shall see how far the pen of the Honourable General directly gave the lie to his tongue.

General Clavering informed the House that he
had never any thing to say to Mrs. Clarke on military affairs, that he did not conceive she had any
interest with the Duke upon these matters. Mrs.
Clarke, on the contrary, who is not now in New-
gate for prevarication, stated, that General Clavering being a distressed man, then a Colonel, she had
spoken to the Duke respecting him; and had a
great deal of difficulty, more so than as to any
other man that she ever applied for in getting any
sort of employment for him. At last she prevailed

upon the Duke to give him a district, and with it he made him a Brigadier-general, entirely through her means. He afterwards asked her to get him a regiment, and fearing they might all be given away before his Royal Highness came to town, she wrote to him when he was reviewing along the coast, and received that letter in which his Royal Highness mentioned General Clavering's name.

Do not these portions of evidences, which we have selected from the minutes of the House in this most important investigation, flash conviction even upon the wilful blindness of the Crown Lawyers. Will they not convince even the stupidity of ignorance? Are they not strong in support of the charges, as proofs of holy writ?

We shall now proceed to the General's correspondence, and mercifully pass over his verbal evidence, which he so officially volunteered in explanation, but which, instead of contradicting the evidence of his benefactress, has, on the contrary, transferred him to garrison duty under Governor Newman.

We shall preface the General's letter to Mrs.
Clarke, upon the new-raised regiments, with the following short note, This note appears first upon the
minutes of the evidence.

———

" *Bishop's Waltham*, 30 *June*, 1804.

" My dear Mrs. C.

" Where your note of Wednesday last has been
travelling, as it only arrived here this morning, I
have no notion, and it had not reached Conduit-
street at five o'clock Wednesday afternoon, when I
quitted town.

" The disappointment is provoking, as I particularly wished to have seen you; but we must console
ourselves in the hope of more fortunate times.

Very truly your's,

M. CLAVERING."

" Mrs. Clarke, 18, Gloucester-Place,
" Portman-Square, London."

We now come to the letter which will explain
the evidence of Mrs. Clarke as to the paragraph

in the Duke's letter, commencing " Clavering is
mistaken, my angel, there are to be no new regiments, &c."

———

" *Bishop's Waltham, 5th Sept.* 1804.

" My Dear Mrs. C.

" You mention that his Royal Highness did not
comprehend my proposal; my idea was this: the
Defence Act, article 30, states, ' that men to be
raised by that act, are not compellable to serve
out of the United Kingdom, and islands immediately attached.' And in 32, ' that they shall not,
remain embodied for more than six months after the
peace.' We have already experienced the fatal necessity of disbanding corps at an apparent conclusion of war, and the mischiefs arising from holding
out temptation to men to extend their services.

" My proposal then was, to raise a battalion for
general and unlimited service, by the voluntary offers
of a stipulated number of men from each regiment of militia, at a certain bounty, in the same

manner as some of our regiments were augment-
ed during the last war. The battalion to be solely
officered from the half-pay list, by which government would at once acquire a certain effective
and well-disciplined force, whose services they can
to any period command, and half-pay to be light-
ened, and the militia colonels have no reason to
growl, since it is determined that their establishment is to be reduced, towards which the men so
volunteering would conduce.

" Should an opportunity occur, do submit the
plan to his Royal Highness, without arguing too
strongly upon it, as he must be tired to death
with proposals; and as I would not appear, even
through so circuitous a channel, to trespass on his
patience, when so recently under an obligation
for my present appointment.

" If you approve of dry reading, get the defence
act to refer to, and do communicate all the good
things in the good town."

The following are a few more Notes, which will sufficiently prove the footing upon which the General stood with his dear Mrs. Clarke.

━━

" Dear Mrs. C.   28 *Sept.*

" I shall not pursue the patridges on the 1st of September; on the contrary, propose being in London in the course of the morning, and beg you will send me word at the Prince of Wales's coffee-house, whether you can receive me in boots about six, or later, if you please.

        " Very truly your's,

             H. M. CLAVERING."

" Mrs. Clarke, 18, Gloucester-place,

  " Portman-square, London."

━━

       Bishop's Waltham 11 *Nov.* 1804.

" My dear Mrs. C.

  " The purport of this is to thank you for your attempt to serve me, tho' unsuccessful, the inclination being the same. On Sunday next I propose being in town, if possible, for one day only. Can you so contrive that we shall meet?

Your's very truly,

H. M. CLAVERING.

" Mrs. Clarke, 18, Gloucester-place,
Portman-square, London."

=====

" *Bishop's Waltham*, Dec. 12, 1804.

" My dear Mrs. C.

" There is a strange report, that some new regiments are about to be raised, which, tho' incredible, I will be obliged to you to ascertain the truth of, and to acquaint me *soon as possible.* W. O. left me this morning for town, to return again next week.

" Very truly your's,

H. M. CLAVERING.

" Mrs. Clarke, 18, Gloucester-place,
" Portman-square, London."

COLONEL WARDLE'S CHARGES.

These, which were eight in number, Mr. Wardle prefaced by observing, That the first establishment under the controul of the Commander in Chief to which he would call the attention of the House, was the *Half-pay Fund*, arising from the sale of commissions vacant, either by death, by promotion, where officers were not allowed to sell, or my dismissals. The legitimate power which the Commander in Chief possessed over this fund was either that of rewarding deserving officers with any of the commissions which fell in, or of causing them to be sold, and the money applied either to the redemption of the Half-pay List, or in aid of the compassionate Fund. If he could prove that commissions, so vacated as he had described, had been sold, and applied to different purposes, he should establish the fact, that the original intention of the Half-pay Fund had been abandoned; for in such cases he should prove, that neither had merit received any reward, the Half-Pay List experienced any reduction, nor the Compassionate Fund obtained any assistence. In the year 1803, his Royal Highness the Commander in Chief took a handsome house in Gloucester-place, engaged a full establishment of servants, and placed at their head a lady of the name of Clarke, whom he should frequently have occasion to mention in the course of what he had to say. And here he trusted that the house would be convinced, from the number of facts which he should have to alledge, and the number of names which he would distinctly and unequivocally declare, that he had not taken up this subject on light grounds.

First Charge.

In the first case that he would submit to the House, Major Tonyn, (then Capt. Tonyn) of the 31st regiment, and Lieutenant Donovan, of the Royal Garrison Battalion, were concerned. The former, as he understood, for he had not the honour of his acquaintance, was a most meritorious officer, and, he trusted, that he should not be considered as casting any reflection on him by stating precisely what had come to his knowledge with respect to

this transaction. Capt. Tonyn, although the son of
a distinguished general, not having been fortunate
enough to obtain the promotion for which he was
anxious, was, by Captain Huxley Sandon, of the
Royal Waggon Train, introduced to Mr. Clarke.
In consequence of that introduction an agreement
was entered into between Mrs. Clarke and Capt.
Tonyn, that on the promotion of the latter to the
majority of the 31st he should pay Mrs. Clarke the
sum of 500l. through the hands of Mr. Donovan.
Before he proceeded it would be necessary to ap-
prise the House who Mr. Donovan was. In the
year 1802 he had been appointed a lieutenant in the
4th Royal Garrison Battalion, and had afterwards
been removed to the 11th Garrison Battalion, in
which he still continued. The House would naturally ask what this gentleman's services have been.
Certainly not of a military nature; for from his first
appointment to the present hour Mr. Donovan had
not gone near his regiment, having, as it were, obtained perpetual leave of absence; a circumstance
at which, when the House became better acquainted
with the kind of services which Mr. Donovan had

actually rendered, they would not be at all surprised. To return to the case which he had been stating, the 500l. lodged by Captain Tonyn with Mr. Donovan was paid into the hands of Mrs. Clarke by Captain Huxley Sandon, and Capt. Tonyn obtained his majority. Now the regulation price of a majority was 1100l.; so that the half-pay fund lost 1100l. for the purpose of putting 500l. in Mrs. Clarke's pocket. This 500l. he could prove was immediately paid by Mrs. Clarke to Mr. Birkett the silversmith, in part of payment for a service of plate sent him to Gloucester-Place, and the deficiency for which was paid by the Commander in Chief. It thus evidently appeared, that his Royal Highness was in this instance an absolute partaker of the benefit derived from this nefarious transaction; and the House would be aware, that to prove the truth or falsehood of the circumstances which he had stated no less than five witnesses might be summoned to their bar, namely, Major Tonyn, Mrs. Clarke, Captain Huxley Sandon, Mr. Donovan, and the executor of Mr. Birkett.

E.

In consequence of the absence of Capt. Sandon
Mr. Wardle commenced with the

Second Charge.

The second case which he should adduce of the
influence possessed by Mrs. Clarke in military matters, was an exchange which took place between
Lieut. Col. Brooke and Lieut. Col. Knight. In this
negociation Dr. Thynne, a medical gentleman of
high respectablity, was concerned. It was agreed
betwixt him and Mrs. Clarke, that if the latter could
effect the wish-for exchange, she should receive an
acknowledgment of 200l. It chanced that just at
this time Mrs. Clarke had strong inclination to make
an excursion into the country: she stated her wishes
to the Commander in Chief, and informed his Royal
Highness that they might be gratified without any
expense to himself, as an opportunity then offered of
obtaining a sum of 200l. provided his Royal Highness would cause the exchange of Col. Brooke and
Col. Knight to take place. On the very next Saturday the exchange of these officers was gazetted.

Of this fact he could prove the reality by the evidence of Lieut. Col. Brooke, Lieut. Col. Knight, Mrs. Clarke, and Dr. Thynne. As a contrast to the facility with which the exchange of these two officers was effected, he would mention a circumstance which had occurred a few weeks ago, and which showed how difficult it was for officers, even of high rank and great respectability, to obtain the most reasonable indulgence, without availing themselves of undue means. Major Macdonald and Major Sinclair, men of high military character, were placed in the following predicament. They were both in bad health. Major Macdonald, with whom the climate of England agreed infinitely better than that of the West Indies, received orders to join his regiment, which was in one of the West India Islands. Major Sinclair, with whom, on the contrary, the climate of the West Indies agreed better than that of England, was most anxious to exchange with Major Macdonald: but notwithstanding the utmost exertions were used by both these officers to obtain an object so desirable by them both, they failed in their endeavours. The Commander

E 2

in Chief forced Major Macdonald to go abroad, he forced Major Sinclair to stay at home, and both had since fallen victims to this cruel arrangement, from not having offered a bribe in a quarter when, perhaps, they were not aware that it would have been unblushingly accepted.

Third Charge.

The third case which he should mention was that of Major Shawe; and on that occasion Mrs. Clarke must have exerted her influence more strongly than usual; for it appeared that Major Shawe was no favourite of the Commander in Chief. Mrs. Clarke and Mr. Shawe, however, soon came to a right understanding, and the latter consented to give the former no less a sum than 1000l. on being appointed deputy barrack-master general at the Cape of Good Hope. Major Shawe's appointment to that situation was in consequence gazetted on the 3d of April, 1807. He immediately paid himself, into Mrs. Clarke's hands, 300l.: soon after he sent her 200l. more, through his uncle Mr. Shawe. For the remaining 500l. Mrs. Clarke applied in vain; and when, after repeated attempts, she found that she had no chance of it, she complained to the Commander in Chief, who felt so much enraged at this circumstance, that he immediately put Major Shawe on half-pay. He (Mr. Wardle) had in his possession a letter of Major Shawe's, complaining heavily of the treatment he had experienced. Mrs. Shawe had also written to Mrs. Clarke, and threatened her and the Commander in Chief with a public exposure of the whole transaction, unless justice were immediately done her husband, but in vain. This case pretty clearly shewed, that Mrs. Clarke's influence extended to the staff as well as to the other departments of the military service; and by reducing an individual from full pay, in consequence alone of his breach of such an iniquitous bargain, the Commander in Chief had made himself a direct party to the transaction.

Fourth Charge.

The fourth case to which he should call the attention of the house, related to a levy under the direction of Col. French. Colonel French applied, in the year 1804, for permission to conduct the levy of a regiment. This levy was set on foot by the influence of Mrs. Clarke, to whom Col. French was introduced by Capt. Huxley Sandon, and an agreement took place, by which it was stipulated that Mrs. Clarke should receive a given sum out of the bounty of each man, and have the patronage of a certain number of officers. This agreement Mrs. Clarke immediately made known to the Duke of York, and then sent Col. French to the Horse Guards to wait on his Royal Highness, where, after several interviews, he succeeded in obtaining his object. As the levy proceeded, Mrs. Clarke received several sums from Col. French, from Capt. Huxley Sandon, and from a Mr. Corri. One sum of 500l. she received by the hands of Mr. Corri, which was paid to him by Mr. Cockayne, a solicitor of eminence in London, employed by Col. French.

Fifth Charge.

The fifth case which he should state it would be necessary for him to revert to Lieutenant Donovan, of the Royal Garrison Battalion, who was the agent of an old officer, a Capt. Tuck, and who had actually given to that officer a written list of the prices at which Mrs. Clarke would engage to procure military promotions, namely, for a majority 900l. for a company 700l. for a lieutenancy 400l. and for an ensigncy 200l. Now, the regulation prices were, for a majority 2,600l. for a company 1500l. for a lieutenancy 550l. and for an ensigncy 400l.; so that the Half-pay List, and the Compassionate Fund must evidently have sustained the most material injury.

Sixth Charge.

The sixth case that he should bring forward was of a still more pointed nature, and bore on the Commander in Chief alone. He was prepared to prove that the Commander in Chief was to have had a loan to a considerable amount from Col. French, or his agent, on conditions of successfully using his influence to procure for Colonel French a large arrear due to him from government, for the very levy

E 4

of which he had already spoken. His Royal Highness did use his influence, but did not succeed, and
did not receive his loan; and it was a fact, that at
that moment there was due from government to Col.
French no less a sum than 3000l.

Seventh Charge.

The seventh case which he should intrude on the
patience of the House, was that of Capt. Maling,
who, being appointed an ensign in the 87th regiment,
on the 28th of November, 1805, was made a lieutenant on the 26th of December, 1806, and obtained
a company in the African corps, on the 15th of
September, 1808.   This African corps, by the way,
was commanded by Col. Gordon, the Duke of York's
private secretary.   Captain Maling was a man of
unexceptionable character; he meant to cast no reflection upon him, but he certainly had had the good
fortune to be a clerk in Mr. Greenwood's office, and
he could prove, that though an ensign in 1805, he
was at Mr. Greenwood's desk in 1807.   But what
was worse, was this, that in three years, without an

hour of actual service, he was put over the heads of all the subalterns in the army, consisting of hundreds of brave men who had long served their country—who had shed their blood in her defence and in the assertion of her glory, and many of whom had even lodged money for the purchase of that promotion which Capt. Maling had thus easily obtained. Whether this was doing justice to the British army or not, he left the House to determine.

This charge was not substantiated.

Eighth Charge.

The eighth case to which he would draw the attention of the House, and on which he could speak from his own knowledge, was, that there existed a public office in the city, open to all comers, where military commissions were offered for sale at the reduced prices which Mrs. Clarke used to exact; and the agents of which declared they were so enabled to offer them by Mrs. Carey, the present favourite of his Royal Highness; and further, that in addition to

commissions in the army, they had the power of procuring all descriptions of places in the church and
state. Nay, those agents had not hesitated to give it
under their own hands, that they were employed by
two of the first officers of his Majesty's administration.*

COL. FRENCH'S LEVY.

Mrs. Clarke's Correspondence with Capt. Sandon.

Mr. Wardle has stated in his charges, that not only
in the army, but in various departments, both in
church and state, places were thus corruptly disposed
of; it has also appeared that writerships and other
appointments under the East India Company; places
in the bank, &c. have also been corruptly sold.

* On Mr. Wardle's being requested to name the agents, he
said the offices he alluded to were held in a court off Thread-
needle-street; that the names of the agents were Haylop and
Pulleu: and that the persons in administration said to be
connected with them were the Lord Chancellor and the Duke
of Portland. The House was convulsed with laughter at the
outrageous absurdity of charges which stumbled all belief.
Prosecutions however have been commenced and some of
the parties will be put upon their trial.

In support of these charges we cannot more effectually convince our readers, than by laying before them the documents which are printed in the minutes.

We shall begin with the correspondence of Capt. Sandon, who we find was introduced to Mrs. Clarke, through Mr. Corri, the musick master, who, as well as Captain Sandon, were clients of Mr. Cockayne, who it will be recollected received the very handsome fee of 200l. from this tormentor of catgut; after which we shall give the correspondence of Mr. Rowland Maltby, of Fishmongers' Hall.

It is necessary here to observe, that Capt. Sandon and Colonel French had applied for a levy through the medium of Mrs. Clarke; the former of whom became acquainted with this lady through the medium of Mr. Cockayne, to both of whom they were clients.

Mrs. Clarke was first known to Mr. Cockayne through Mr. Corri, the music master.

The terms of Mrs. Clarke's interference were to have been at first 500l.; there was however some subsequent alterations, and she was to have received a guinea additional for every man raised.

Mrs. Clarke, who, as will appear from the correspondence was extremely short of cash, says she was teazed every day about this levy. Colonel French complaining of other parties having larger bounties than were allowed to his levy, which hurt his recruiting very much, was desirous of having his bounties increased.

The bounty was originally *thirteen guineas* which through the interest of Mrs. Clarke were increased to nineteen. During this period Mrs. Clarke says that she was teazed every day, and she always told, or gave H. R. H. Col. French's notes.

It will be recollected that the evidence of that much injured young female strongly comes in aid of this assertion of Mrs. Clarke's; for about this period it was, that Miss Taylor, as nearly as she could recollect, stated, that the Duke of York said, I am *continually worried* by Col. French—he *worries me continually about the levy business, and is always wanting something more in his own favour.* Turning to Mrs. Clarke, I think, she states, he said, " *How does he behave to you, Darling?*" or some such kind words as he used to use; that was all that was said.

On being further questioned, Do you recollect any thing further passing than what you have stated? Mrs. Clarke replied, " Middling; not very well." That was all that she said. The Duke said, " *Master French must mind what he is about, or I shall cut up him and his levy too.*"

Mrs. Clarke says she stated to the Commander in Chief that she was to derive pecuniary advantages from this levy, and he promised her that Colonel French should have a levy—that she received in consequence 500 guineas, bank notes making up the sum of guineas, 500l. of which she paid to Birkett, on account for a service of plate, and his Royal Highness told her he paid the remainder by his own bills.

This fact was proved by John Messenger, assistant to Mr Birkett, who stated that certain bills drawn by Clarke on Farquhar were taken up by the Duke of York—that they received on the 19th September, a draft of the duke of York's, dated on the 18th of January, 1806, for 400l, dated forward three months, and due on the 18th February. He also stated other bills drawn by Bell on Millard, and one drawn by bell on Pritchard, for 100l. each; and a promissory note made by the Duke of York, payable to Parker, dated on the 8th of February, at four months, for 230l.

The bill for 400l. was taken up in 1805. Mr. Parker had Mrs. Clarke's jewels as a security for these advances.

The payment of these bills were afterwards proved by a clerk in the house of Messrs. Coutts and Co. H. R. H's bankers.

We have in some degree digressed to connect the links of evidence, and give our readers a bird's eye view of the whole of the transaction relative to Col. French's levy, which Col. Gordon complained of was so exceedingly unproductive, that it must be discontinued.

We now proceed to Captain Sandon's correspondence.

No. 1.

" Sir,

" Perhaps you may have forgotten there was such a person in existence as the writer. I have been in the country for a year and a half, and I am but just returned from it, to remain in town; and I should feel myself particularly obliged if you will favour me *with your friend Colonel French's address*, or his agent in the inn, in Holborn, which has slipped my memory. Pray forgive the trouble, and believe me your most obedient

MARY ANN CLARKE."

Captain Sanden,
Royal Waggon Drivers.

No. 2.

" 14, *Bedford-Place, Russel-Square,*
July 23.

" Dear Sir,

" On Saturday I was favoured with your answer, but as I have removed from Hollis-Street to
this place, to save you the trouble of calling there,
these lines are addressed you.

" I am now with my mother, and, I fear, for
the whole of the summer. *I did not want any thing*
of French but to ask him a question.

I am, dear Sir,
Your obliged, &c. &c.

MARY ANN CLARKE."

": Captain Sandon, Royal Waggon, Train.
Twopenny Post unpaid, Tottenham C. R."

No. 3.

" Mrs. Clarke will be glad of a call from Captain Sandon, if he is returned to town, to day or to-morrow.

" *Gloucester-Place, Friday.*

" Colonel Sandon, Westminster Bridge."

———

No. 4.

" I am thoroughly convinced of the *money being too trifling.* I have mentioned it to a person who knows the full value of these things; so you may tell *Bacon* and *Spedding* they must give each of them more *two hundred,* and the captains must give me *fifty* each more. I am now offered *eleven hundred* for an older officer.

" I must have an answer this evening to this, as I am to speak with him on it. I have mentioned as your being concerned for me. I go to the little theatre this evening."

Let us pause a moment, to reflect upon the mode in which this traffic is carried on, and we may confidently observe that these written documents will throw more light upon this subject than all the *viva voce evidence* introduced at the bar of the House, although that evidence strictly corroborated the written documents, and the written documents in return contributed to form one close, compact and solid body of evidence.

Mrs. Clarke applies to Captain Sandon for the address of Colonel French, of whom she says she wants nothing but *to ask a question.*

In the two last letters we find her chaffering about the price of commissions—the money, as she has been informed by a person who knew *the full* value of those things (possibly Mr. Donovan) was too little, " so *Bacon* and *Spedding* must give each of them more *two hundred,* and the captains must give *fifty* each more."

" I am now offered *eleven hundred for an older officer.*"

‹ Does not the insulted spirit of the English reader flame with indignation at the concluding part of this letter—Does not the experienced officer, whose only interest is perhaps the regulated price, which he can muster with difficulty, by sacrificing the comforts of gray-headed parents, tremble at such abuse? Will not his exertions be paralysed, and will he not sink into all the apathy of despair, when he finds himself thus sacrificed to the avarice and caprice of this Petticoated Field-Marshal and Commander in Chief; although, perhaps, the veteran candidate might have acquired his scars in the field, or wasted his health in the sultry and pestilential climes of India.

To the immortal honor, however, of Colonel Wardle, and the patriotic Members of the House of Commons, this abuse is at length checked, and we trust, by perseverance, will be eventually suppressed.

The postscript of this letter carries something also expressive at once of impatience and mystery.

" *Must* have an answer this evening, as she is to see HIM *upon it*;"

Nec Deus intersit dignus nisi vindice nodus.

HIM!!! – *Who* is this stupendous stranger? She is to see him *upon it*.

Upon what?——Will any one doubt the answer.

The next letter introduces Mr. Corri, who, the reader will recollect, talked of long nosed, and ugly faces, destroyed Mr. Clarke's letters, and was the worthy and liberal associate with that unblemished solicitor, Mr. Cockayne.

Prostitutes, fiddlers, usurers, pawnbrokers, attorneys, army-brokers, and H. R. H. the Field-Marshal of Great Britain. Mercy on us, what an heterogenous mixture! but in these times

" Motley's your only wear."

This makes O'Keefe's expression no joke:

" Alexander, Julius Cæsar, Wat Tyler, and Jack Straw."

The following letter will also prove to the people of England, how votes, upon particular occasions, are obtained from their representatives!!

No. 5.

" Colonel Sandon,

" Will you, my good Sir, drop me a line on Monday morning, saying if you have been able to *influence any person who is with Pitt* to attend the House on Monday, *to give his vote.*

" I have this morning received the inclosed from Corri, and where he marks under, he alludes to your business, and as *I know* he is a story-teller, I send you his letter. I am, &c·

" M. A. CLARKE."

" Col. Sandon, No. 15, Bridge Street,
Westminster Bridge."

" *Pitt's Motion, &c. Corri.—complainant.*"

So here we have corruption with a vengeance— here was corruption in the army to be used

for corrupting the representatives of the people;
to pollute and poison the very source and fountain.
which can alone purge the *Augean* Stable, and re-
store the country to a state of sound and pristine
health; but the Guardian Angel of Great Britain
has detected the corruption, and we trust he has not
interposed his Ægis too late for the salvation of the
country.

We shall proceed to give the following letters
without any comment; they will sufficiently speak
for themselves; and we trust, that the whole of the
proceedings in this most important investigation will
prove, that instead of the conspiracy against the
House of Brunswick, there has been a conspiracy
not only against the army, but the Constitution of
England.

No. 6.

" Dear Sir,

"'He will do it—— so let the proposals be sent in.
by when he gets to town, which will be as soon as
you get this, *for one thousand* at first.——*The Duke*

of Cambridge has already four thousand. You have not any occasion to be very particular as *to their being Protestants, for I don't think it of any consequence to him !!!* I think you had better attend him on Tuesday, to ask his opinion of the papers sent in on Saturday, as I told him I had seen the proposals, which you intended *to alter* and leave that evening.——Pray when you go put on a *nice pair* of boots, and let it be about half past 3.

"Adieu—burn this."

"*Mrs. Clarke's Letter, relative to German Levy.*"

———

No. 7.

"Can you give me a call to-day about one or two, or about five? I wish to see you much. Tell Spedding to write in for what he wants, as *the D. says that he is much the best. Can you get half a dozen or so that want interest?—I want money,* which is more imperious. This is what I want to see you upon, so you had better see Gilpin first. What is become of Bacon?

"Colonel Sandon,

"*Interest and Money.*"

No. 8.

" Dear Sir,

" Pray do something for me soon as possible; the *Duke told me this morning you must get on faster with your men;* he has written to town for that purpose. You had better send me the exact number of all you have sent, and I will shew it him.

" Colonel Sandon.

" He complains of the slowness of recruiting the levy."

=====

No. 9.

" I send this by a servant to Hampton, hoping you will get it sooner.

" Dear Sir, " *Thursday morning.*

" The Duke has neither seen General Tonyn nor his son—his son he does not know, and it is six months since he saw the General. He has ordered him to be gazetted, and is fearful it will be done ere he can stop it—he will be at the office to-morrow, and if not too late, will stop it. He assured me *it was entirely owing to me that he thought to do the best by putting* him where two others Majors have left and he would of course be *two steps higher.*

" I hope to see you to-morrow, when you will be able to give me the answer from Tonya ; shall be in town about 5.

" The King and all the Family are coming to visit the Duke, *being his birth-day ! ! !* Full of compliment you see.

" 12 o'clock, 17th August, 1804.
" Colonel Sandon, No. 15, Bridge-street,
    Westminster Bridge, London."

    " 12 o'clo   " Two-Penny POST
August 17, 1804, Noon.   Twickenham."

No. 10.

" Mrs. Clarke's compliments await Col. Sandon, thinks it best for him *not to come to her box this evening, as Greenwood goes with both the Dukes this evening, and of course will watch where your eyes direct now and then* ; and should he see and know Colonel

S———, may make some remark by saying or talking of the *Levy* business, and it may be hurtful to his and Mrs. C.'s future interests.

" 9th Oct. 1804.   See Richard Cœur de Lion.
" Col. Sandon, No. 8, Lyon's Inn.

═══

No. 11.

" Dear Sir,

" Capt'n Tonyn cannot be made this month as I expected; the D. tells it will be at least three weeks, he having so much to do in reviewing: and there are some other promotions *now* to take place— *however the thing is done.*

" The little boy will be attended to.   On Monday I shall go to Vauxhall with a party, when perhaps I shall have the pleasure of seeing you; it is the only night this summer I shall have the opportunity, as on that night *he is obliged to attend the House of Lords, as they expect a great fight on Pitt's motion.* I shall at some time take an opportunity of mentioning your majority.   I asked *him what he thought of you ?* A D - - - clever fellow——*You are to have the bounty that Pitt is to give to the line*, so that every thing goes on well.   I told him I should see you at Vauxhall on Monday.——I am now at the end of my paper, so shall say adieu.

" M. A. C."

" He says General Tonyn is *a stupid old fellow.*

" Relative to the majority and advance of bounty.

" Colonel Sandon, No. 15, Bridge-street,
    Westminster Bridge."

—

No. 12.

" *Weybridge, Friday Noon.*

" Dear Sir,   *".burn this*

" I *have mentioned the Majority to the* D——, he is very agreeable to it ; it is the nephew of the Gen'l; his son purchased a company last week—— Do you think it at all possible to oblige me on Monday with *one hundred*, I shall be in town Sunday.   If I had had the pleasure. of seeing you at the races, I

intended to have *painted you out to the D.*——
If you are in town, will you have the goodness to
send a line in answer. It will oblige much your
most

" Obedt. M. A. C."

" Colonel Sandon, No. 13, Bridge-street,
   Westminster Bridge, London."

" *Majority, June 8th, 1804.*"

C   4
JUN 9,   ESHER
1804.   16

No. 13.

" *Thursday.*

" I'll tell you, Col. French, you can materially
serve me, by *giving me a bill for two hundred,* for *two
months or ten weeks.*

" I shall at all times be happy to serve you in any
way. I like Capt. Sandon extremely, *I suppose he is
the managing person ?*   " M. A. C."

" Drop me a line in answer.

" 1st letter from Mrs. Clarke."

No. 14.

" Mrs. Clarke's compliments attend on Colonel Sandon, will be glad to see him to-morrow from eleven till one.

Thursday, Feb. 28."

Two-Penny POST,   " Colonel Sandon,
Coventry-street.   " No. 8, Lyon's Inn,
                                        " Wych-street."

No. 15.

" My dear Sir,

" I am vexed to death, you will know the state of my finances, and I hit upon *Spedding for Tuesday,* when, behold, the Regt. he is in did their exercise so bad that *the Duke swore at them very much, and has stopped the promotion of every one in it!* He said so much to the Col. (Wemyss, I think) that if he had been a gentleman he would have given up—but he intends looking over the memorial to day, as S. has not been long in that Regt. and he is an old officer. So that you see *if he gets his promotion, how very much he ought to be indebted to my good offices.* I

к 3.

must beg hard for him, the Duke is very angry with you; for when he last saw you, you promised him 300 foreigners, and you have not produced one. *O, yes, Master Sandon is a pretty fellow to depend on.* I wish I had hit upon Eustace first. I told you, I believe, *that they must be done gradually, his clerks are so cunning.* Get Spedding to write out a list of his services, and send it to me *as a private thing to.* shew him, not addressed to any one.——Adieu."

No. 16.

" Dear Sir,

" I asked this morning if he had *himself* read those papers I gave him of the Col.'s, he said that he had; but that he still asked so much more than other men, that he could not think of closing with him: however let him send again, as *perhaps he forgets his papers in his hurry*, especially as he had those at home.

" I cannot do myself the pleasure of being
[*torn*]

No. 17:

" Dear Sir,

" I shall esteem it a favour if you will make *im-mediate* enquiry about a lieutenancy, (I understand there are two to be disposed in the 14th light dragoons,) as *Charles Thompson* is determined to quit his next week, and I wish for his own sake that he goes direct to the other, as the Duke might be displeased with any one being idle at this critical moment. If you are in the way I shall expect a line, just to say if you think it possible for him to purchase so soon. His R. H. goes out of town to Chelmsford Saturday, and returns to town to his office 3 o'clock Tuesday.

" M. A. C."

" Colonel Sandon,
No. 15, Westminster-Bridge,
Bridge-street, Westminster."

We shall only here observe, that Charles Thompson is the brother of Mrs. Clarke, who was honorably acquitted upon her evidence of a charge in a court-martial held at Colchester.

———

No. 18.

" Dear Sir,

" Major Taylor has proposed to do something in the Irish levies for his lt.-colonelcy, but it will be effected ; the friend of ours says he will let him pur-chase, although he is so young a Major, but this you know is nothing to us ; so do you see him, and if you enter upon the same terms as before, I think I shall be able *to teaze him out of it ;* let me know the result of it as soon as possible.

" Do you think it all possible for you and French to let me draw a bill on you for 200l. I am so dreadfully distressed I know not which way to turn myself, and before that will be due you are aware of what is to be done for me in that negocia-tion. *Thank you for the pig,* it was the most deli-cate thing of the kind possible. Adieu.

" Dear Sir, I am,

" *Wednesday, Jan. 30.*" &c. &c.

No. 19.

" Dear Sir,

" As I leave town on Monday evening, and running short of cash, will you be kind enough to send me by Monday the hundred pounds.

" Colonel Sandon."　　　　　" M. A. C."

———

No. 20.

" Dear Sir,

" Most unfortunately Lord Bridgewater has asked for the vacancy, 'ere indeed it was one, so that that is done   [torn]   ; but H. R. H. will let me know if he can at 4 o'clock. He does not go out of town, as intended, to-morrow, on account of his Majesty having been insulted yesterday, and still fears it. I have a bill due either on Saturday or Monday, I know not which day; can you get me the *five hundred guineas?* He has been signed, and will be in the gazette to-morrow; you know who I mean.

" Instead of a 60-guinea harp let it be 100, *as I have told him you was going to present me one,* therefore it must be very elegant.

" Tell Zimmences he shall have   [*torn*]   he wishes for 700 guineas *not*   [*torn*]   he shall have it in a month.

" Don't fail burning my scribble soon as read.

" I do not go out of town to-morrow.

" Colonel Sandon, No. 15, Bridge-street,
  " Westminster: or Duke-street,
  " Adelphi, No. 9, Office."

———

No. 21.

" Dear Sir,   " *Thursday.*

" I am extremely sorry to inform you (for the poor boy's sake) but it is impossible to admit him, as he has that misfortune you mentioned of being *one-eyed.* Do you think it possible to get me a

vote on Monday for Pitt's motion? It will, if carried,
be of some consequence to us hereafter; try all
you can.

"I remain, dear Sir, Your's, &c.

"M. A. CLARKE."

"Colonel Sandon,
"Bridge-street, No. 15, Westminster-bridge.

"Send me an answer."

No. 22.

"What you ask will be at your service, and the
letter will be at your office Monday morning.

"Colonel Sandon."

No. 23.

"Mrs. Clarke will be glad to see Captain Sandon
to-morrow, before twelve o'clock, if he is in town; if
not, Monday at five.—

"Friday, 1 o'clock, 6 JY.
"1804. N. T.
"Colonel Sandon, No. 5, Bridge-street,
"Westminster-bridge."
2 TWO Py POST unpaid.

No. 24.

" Dear Sir,

" There is not any such thing in contemplation as the written question. Will you again ask about *an India Lieutenancy*? As the Duke assures me there are two for sale. In consequence of what I mentioned to him of Kenner, he has made many enquiries, and finds him to be a black sheep; he offered to bribe Col. Gordon a few days since ! !

" M. A. C."

" Colonel Sandon."   48th Antedate.

No. 25.

" Dear Sir,

" 'Ere I leave town I scratch a few lines, begging you to be on your guard in every point; Lst of *my name* in particular, for the future never breathe it. I am confident you have a number of enemies, for yesterday the —— was assailed from seven or eight different persons with invective against you. He is a little angry at something; yet will not tell it.

me. I think this fellow Kenner tries his friends; they laid fine complaints against you—did you tell Zimmenees that as soon as Tonyn was gazetted you would get him done, in the same way, and that I was the person? Let me see you on Tuesday.

" Adieu, I am interrupted."

No. 26.

" My dear Sir,

" Be so good as to look at the gazette to-morrow eveng. as I rather expect some of the names to be inserted. I have others which I assure you upon my honour. The present for my trouble for the majority is *seven hundred guineas*, so if you have any more this must be the same. I shall be in town Monday, if you will have any thing to communicate. I remain,

" Dear Sir, your's, &c. &c.

" Friday Eveng. 7 o'Clock,   " M.A.C.
    " 28 Sp. 1804 Nt.
" Colonel Sandon, No. 8, Lyon's Inn,
    " Wyche-street, Strand."
    Two-Penny POST.

No. 27.

" Dear Sir,   22d—8th.

" I make a mistake, it is the 22d regiment Mr.
Thompson is to purchase into, or the 8th. Shall
I see you to-day?

M.A.C.

" What is Thompson to say to his Colonel?
Charles Farquhar Thompson, 13 to 8 or 22d.
" Colonel Sandon, 15, Bridge-street,

" Westminster."

No. 28.

" I gave the papers to his Royal Highness; he
read them while with me; said he still thought
men high; but that an answer would be left at his
office as the way of business.

" I told him if any was appointed, to give the
Colonel the preference. Burn this soon as read.
I do not comprehend exactly what you mean by
five other things; I do not think it possible.

No. 29.

" Can you send me one hundred pounds to-day ; and let me see you to-morrow morning.

" Colonel Sandon."   " M. A. C."

———

No. 30.

" Dear Sir,   *Friday.*

" Will you go to the Horse-guards for me to-day, and leave a proper letter as coming from Charles Thompson, asking for leave of absence for a fortnight; but if his service should be wanted he would join immediately: if you know any belonging to the adjutants, you could get it by to-morrow.

" Colonel Sandon."   M. A. C.

———

No. 31.

" I have a letter which says you are a *money-lender, in collegue with a notorious man, called Dell!* I wish to show it you.

" I hope you will attend the Duke to-day, as Clinton. leaves him on Thursday, and he has all the writings for you in hand: he will not leave his office till six.—

" I shall be glad of *a hundred guineas*, if possible, this week. Saturday week Tonyn will be gazetted. How comes on French? call to-morrow, if possible..
" Colonel Sandon, 15, Bridge-street,.
        Westminster."

No. 32.

" As your servant has called, and fearing you may not have my letter, beg you to see the Duke to-day at all events, or else things will be longer about, as Colonel Gordon takes Clinton's place on Thursday."

No. 33.

" Dear Sir,
" " Pray what can Spedding mean by asking on Thursday, through General Tonyn, for leave to go

on half-pay? 'Tis odd behaviour, and you must think that *some* one. thinks me used very ill; of course, till this is fully explained, I shall drop all thoughts of any thing else.

" Saturday.   " I remain your's,

" Colonel Sandon."   " M.A.C.

No. 34.

" Sir,

" I am exactly treated as I have been led to, believe, from more than one quarter, but will thank you to send me Colonel French's address to-day, before the post goes out. I have nothing to do with your agent, you know.

       " I remain, Sir, your most obedient,

                 M.A.C."

No. 35.

" As Colonel Sandon did not call according to promise, Mrs. C. hopes he will have the goodness to send her a bill at two monts, in the morning; surely

all things will be settled before that becomes due.
Mrs. C. hopes he will not disappoint.

" Monday.

" Colonel sandon, Lyon's Inn,

" Wyche-street"

No. 36.

" Sir,

" You have disappointed me dreadfully, a bill of
one hundred at three months is useless, it must be
for two hundred at three months, or one at six weeks

for one hundred

or two months. I beg you to return it by the
bearer, as I mentioned my situation to you. Word
it thus——I promise to pay to six weeks or two
months after date, pay Mr. Thompson, or order, the
sum of one hundred pounds for value received.

" Pray let me have it this evening at all events.

" M.A.C.

No. 37.

" Mrs. Clarke's compliments attend Captain Sandon, will feel herself much obliged if he will do his best for Thompson in the recruiting business, as on his getting the men early will give him first rank.

" Mrs. C. has not been able to get an answer from H. R. H. about Taylor.

" Dec. 26.

" Colonel Sandon, No. 8, Lyon's Inn,

  " Wych Street."

2 Two Py. POST.   Dec. 26th, 1804.

 Blandford.   Dec. 26, 1804.

   J. S. 7 o'clock, 26 Dec. 1804. N. n.

No. 38.

" Mrs. C. must again intreat the assistance of Colonel S——. He well knows she has always done as he has wished her to do.

" Colonel Sandon, No. 8, Lyon's Inn,

  " Wych Street."

No. 39.

" I am told an answer is left out for Colonel French, at the office, and that now he has dropped three guineas per man.—

" I am not aware of what the answer is intended to convey.

" Mr. Corri.   [torn]   k will.

No. 40.

" I hope you will not disappoint me, as on you alone depend my hopes of taking up a bill over due. " Colonel Sandon."

No. 41.

" 2, *Westbourne Place, Sloan Square, Dec. 2d.*

" Dear Sir,

" Let me know where you are, and I have not

the least doubt but I can serve you essentially, and remain as ever your friend.

" MARY ANN CLARKE."
" Captain Sandon, Waggon Train, Spain.
" By Messrs. Greenwood and Co. Lyon's
    Inn, Strand, London."

Portsmouth, Jan. 29, 1809.

2d Dec. 1808.
    G. Jan. 30, 1809.

———

MR. DONOVAN'S CORRESPONDENCE.

In the former documents, viz. Captain Sandon's correspondence, we have confined ourselves to the corrupt disposal of commissions in the army, we shall now step a little further into the interior of this warehouse, where we shall find not only commissions in the army, but places in the customhouse, and even preferments in the church, viz. the Deaneries of Hereford and Gloucester; one for the Rev. Dr. Glasse, we firmly believe without his knowledge or privity—the other, the Rev. Dr. Basely, *Chaplain to the Duke of Gloucester*, and who, Mr. Donovan says, *is recommended by so many*

persons of fashion, Bishops of Norwich and Salisbury, &c. about whom *the ladies are so very
anxious.*

———

No. 1.

" Charles-street, St. James's-square,
October 20th, 1808.

" Dear Madam,

" The *Deanery of Hereford is vacant,* and in the
sole gift of the Duke of Portland; can you procure
it for the *Rev. G. H. Glasse?* I would myself unknown to him, give 1000l. for it. It must be
filled by next Saturday, at least, so a gentleman,
who has just given me the information, said, Mr.
G. is my most particular friend, and I would make
great sacrifices to serve him; he is not in town at
present. I can with confidence assure you he is a
very good scholar, a man of good fortune, and an
extraordinary kind *friend,* of excellent connections,
well known to the Dukes of Cumberland and
Cambridge. He is rector of Hanwell, Middlesex.
His town house No. 10, Sackville Street.

" " The money will be deposited on Wednesday next, for the *Landing Waiter's Place.*

" *An Inspector of the Customs,* whose duty is rowing in a boat about the river, visiting and placing officers on board different ships, is about to be superanuated, the salary is 400 per annum; I am applied to for the appointment, on the resignation taking place; 1000l. *is offered for it.*

" Your's very truly,

" Mrs. Clarke."   J. DONOVAN.

No. 2.

" *Charles-street, St. James's-square,*
October 8th, 1808."

" Dear Madam,

" Some friends of the Rev. T. Baseley, M. A. are extremely desirous of procuring for him promotion in the church; and it appears to them a very favourable opportunity, the *vacancy of the Deanery of Salisbury,* to make application to the Duke of Portland; and in order to secure an interest without his knowledge of a party of Ladies, at the head of whom is *Lady Cardigan, have subscribed a sum of money,* 3000 *guineas,* which is ready to be deposited to carry into execution their intended plan.

Mr. Basely is well known to his Grace, and was particularly recommended to her Majesty by Lady Cardigan, on the publication of his pamphlet, ' *The Claims of the Roman Catholics constitutionally considered, &c. &c.*' This chaplain to the Duke of Gloucester, and the Bishop of Lincoln, went *with his Grace* upon some occasion to serve the Marquis of Titchfield; would be very strongly recommended *by many persons of fashion, the Bishops of Norwich and Salisbury.* I have a letter from each to Mr. Baseley in my possession, which would shew the estimation in which he is held by them. *The Ladies are very anxious,* and at the same time desirous that he should not know through what channel the money is raised, much less the application, nor do they wish to know any thing further than that he shall succeed, and then *to agreeably surprise him;* or rather that his Grace, without any preface should have the whole merit of having selected *so worthy a man to fill the vacancy.* Your answer will oblige,

" Your's very truly,

" J. DONOVAN."

" Lord M. and Mrs. Jn. are in town."

No. 3.

" *Charle's-street, St. James's-square, Nov. 16, 1808.*"

" Dear Madam,

" The place of *Inspector of the Customs is now vacant by the death of Mr. Booty,* and I learn that THE QUEEN *and the Duke of Dorset* are about to apply for it. I hope you will procure it for *Mr. Henry Tobin,* the gentleman you were so good to say you would serve when an opportunity offered. I will do myself the pleasure of waiting on you whenever you will appoint on the subject. *Can you procure the paymastership to a second battalion for* 500*l.*   " Your's very truly,

" J. DONOVAN."

" Mrs. Clarke."

G

No. 4.

" Dec. 14, 1808.

" Dear Madam,

" I regret much that I had not the pleasure to see you on Saturday evening. It was the only time I had been out since Tuesday, and I have suffered considerably in consequence, from my wound.

" I am daily applied to for the particulars of the *appointment at Savannah La Marr. Is it a Surveyor of Customs and Landing Waiter? Is the salary* 1300l. per annum, or how much is the salary, and from what do the perquisites arise? Is the 1300*l.* *sterling or Jamaica currency?* What is the duty? Can you procure the Landing Waiter's place, in January next?

" *The Paymaster's second battalion?*

" Relative to the *letters*, I am in part ready, and wish to *consult with you* relative to them. I shall be at home this evening, and, if able to bear the motion of a carriage, dine in your neighbourhood to-morrow.

" I remain, dear Madam,

" Your's very truly,

" J. DONOVAN."

" Mrs. Clarke."

No. 5.

" *Charle's-street, St. James's-square,*

Dec. 23d, 1808.

" Dear Madam,

" I am *daily plagued about the Savannah La Mar appointment;* also respecting the Landing Waiter's, the 2d Battn. Paymastership, and the Commissary-ship. Pray let me hear from, or see you, on the subject of the Savannah business particularly.

" Mrs. Howes requested me to thank you in her name for your kindness, and have got into disgrace

G 2

for not having done so sooner, and for not letting her know when you call'd last.

"Your's very truly,

"J. DONOVAN."

"Mrs. H. sends her compts."

"Mrs. Clarke."

———

The following are letters from Mrs. Clarke to Donovan, which, as it will be observed, were received after the charges.

[The witness delivered in two letters, which were read, dated the 28th of January, and the 1st of February, 1809.]

"Dear Sir,

"I am much mortified in seeing, in this day's paper, the free use of your name and mine in the debate last night. I however took an opportunity of seeing Mr. Wardle on the subject, and I find he is by no means so ill disposed as his speech seemed to evince; but he tells me, that as I have committed myself and my papers, he is determined to make

every possible use of them, that to him seems proper. I must be candid, and tell you, that in order
to facilitate some negociations, I had given him a
few of your letters. In one *you speak of the Queen,
in another of the two deaneries.* The deaneries of
Hereford and Salisbury, the former for Dr. Glasse,
and the latter for *Baseley.* As to myself, I must of
course speak the truth, as I shall be put on oath.
Let me persuade you, if called on, to keep to the
truth, as I am convinced you will; but I mean the
whole truth, as to what has passed formerly between
yourself and me. I have a thousand thanks for
your being so quiet upon the 130; you shall have it
the moment my mother comes from Bath. I fear, if
you are backward, Wardle will expose the whole of
the letters he has to the House.

> " Your's, truly,
>> " M. A. CLARKE."

" Saturday evening."

" In order to relieve your mind, I send my servant,
though late."

Indorsed:

" Recd. 28th Jany. 1809, late at night."

Wednesday Morning, Feb. 1, 1809."

" Dear Sir,

" I yesterday saw Mr. Wardle; he had a letter from your friend Glass, begging him not to take
any business in hand, where his name is mentioned;
and he asks for you also.   He was tutor to Wardle.
Now Mr. Wardle assures me, by every thing honourable, that if you speak candidly and fairly to the fact
of Tonyns, he will ask nothing more; and if he has
been at all intemperate with your name, he will do it
every justice.   *Take my advice and do it;* it cannot
injure you.   I understand your friend *Tuck* some
months ago put a friend of his in possession of
Tonyn's business; and yesterday a man of the name
of Finnerty gave him a case, which, he says, he had
from you, of a Captain Trotter and another.   Of
course you will not mention my telling you this.   I
wish from my soul Mr. Wardle had taken it up less
dispassionately, he might have done more good.   Why

do you not send me a line?   I dare say Clavering is hugging himself, as he did not send the recommenda-tion.

"Your's, &c.

"M. A. C."

━━━

We now proceed to the would-be Dean of Salis-bury, or some other deanery—Dr. Baseley, good easy man, ignorant of the secret agency of Mr. Donovan, and his female friends, to give him an agreeable sur-prise, by promoting him without his knowledge, applies himself personally to the Duke of Portland, and actually offered his Grace a bribe of 3000l. for the deanery of Salisbury, which was treated as it ought, by acquainting the Bishop of London, whose recommendation was rather more *unfashionable* than that of the Bishops of Norwich and Salisbury.

The following letter was read by the Marquis of Titchfield in the House of Commons.

" *Norfolk-Street, Grosvenor-Square.*

" My Lord Duke,

" I wished particularly to see your Grace upon *the most private business.* I cannot be fully open by letter. The object is, *to solicit your Grace's recommendation to the deanery of Salisbury, or some other deanery, for which the most ample pecuniary remuneration I will instantly give a Draft to your Grace.*

For Salisbury, three thousand pounds. I hope your Grace will pardon this, and instantly commit these lines to the flames. *I am now writing for the benefit of administration, a most interesting pamphlet.* Excuse this openness; and I remain your Grace's

" Most obedient and

" obliged Servant,

" T. BASELEY."

" I will attend your Grace whenever you may appoint, but sincerely beg your Grace's secresy."

Indorsed:

Delivered by the writer himself to my servant, on Tuesday, 3 Jan. 1809, at Bn. House, P."

This letter, said the Marquis of Tichfield, was delivered by the writer himself, and is indorsed by the Duke of Portland, the 3d of January in the present year. Upon receiving this letter, my noble relation, finding that the writer of it was gone, gave particular orders that Mr. Baseley never should be admitted into his house, and the same day wrote a letter to the Bishop of London, of which the following was the copy, inclosing also Baseley's letter.

"*Burlington House*, Tuesday, 3d Jan. 1808

" My Lord,

" The person by whom the note inclosed was left at my house this morning, being possessed, as I understand, of one, if not of two chapels in your Lordship's diocese, I consider it to be incumbent upon me, from the sense I have of the duty I owe to the public, as well as from my respect for your Lordship, not to suffer you to remain uninformed of it; and I accordingly take the liberty of laying it before you.

" I have reason to believe that the note is written by the person whose name is subscribed to it, as I have heretofore received notes or letters from him, the writing of which, to the best of my recollection, very much, if not exactly, resembles that of the note enclosed; and one, if not more of which, was written at my house in consequence of my declining to see him. The note inclosed, however, he brought with him; and on my desiring to be excused seeing him, he gave it to my servant, and immediately left my house.

"As I have no copy of the note, I must desire your Lordship to return it to me."

Indorsed:
" To the Lord Bishop of London, 3d Jan. 1809."

———

Answer by the Bishop of London.

" *Fulham-House,* Jan. 5, 1809.

" My Lord,

" It is impossible for me to express the astonishment and indignation which were excited in my mind, by the perusal of the letter which your Grace has done me the honour of enclosing; a mark of your attention, for which I must beg you to accept my best thanks.

" It is too true that this *wretched creature Baseley has one if not two chapels in my diocese.* I have long known him to be *a very weak man*, but till this insufferable insult upon your Grace, *I did not know he was so completely wicked, and so totally void of all principle:* and as your Grace is in possession of the most incontestible proofs of his guilt, you will, I trust, *inflict upon him the disgrace and the punishment he so richly deserves.*

" I have the honour to be,

" With the highest respect,

" My Lord,

" Your Grace's most humble

" and obedient servant,

" B. LONDON."

@ 6

MR. ROWLAND MALTBY'S CORRESPON DENCE.

We now proceed to another branch of this general agency, and submit to our readers, with a very few observations, the correspondence of Mr. Rowland Maltby, of Fishmonger's Hall, who, Mrs. Clarke observes, was her *Duke of Portland*.

This correspondence relates to negociations for places of different descriptions, and arrangements relative to the deposit of money for places in the War-Office, cadetships, &c.

Omnia venalia Romæ.

No. 1.

"Dear Madam,   *Friday Morn.*

" The regiment for Mr. Williams is going to *India*; this is lucky; therefore, let him immediately provide the needful, and I will arrange in *what* way it is to be deposited. Have you written to him, as no time is to be lost.

" As to the 2d battak in the gentleman here and prepared?

"Your's truly,

"R. M."

"Pray give me a line in ans."

No. 2.

" Dear Madam,

" If you can *by any means forward the adjustment* of Mr. Manners' account as to his claims respecting the 26th regt. whilst in Egypt, of which the late General Manners was the Colonel,

" You will much oblige, dear Madam,

"Your's truly,

" *July* 28th.　　　　" R. MALTBY."

" I don't know your true address I called in Holles-street, a few days ago, and found you were gone."

No. 3.

" My dear Madam,　　　　*Saturday Ev.*

" I thank you very much for your kind attention;

you would be *quite a treasure in every way to any Secretary of State.*

"I am as anxious as you can be, that there may be no disappointment in the Commssp.; and I am goading the parties every day.

"You say nothing of the P——ship 2d batt.; is the party ready?

"When do you leave B—— place?

"I am, dear Madam,

"Your's, truly,

"R. M."

———

No. 4.

"Dear Madam,

"If I have not the letter of recommendation immediately, and the money ready, I fear it will be lost. I understand the regiment is *very respectable,* but I do not know the county yet.

"Remember the Paymastership.

"Your's truly,

"Friday Aftern.   R. M."

No. 5.

" Dear Madam, *May 20th.*

" Mr. M. is not, I believe, in this country, but far distant ; so it will not answer to send your letter. Shall I enquire for the object you mention ? What *rank*, and *what* shall I propose for it ?

" *Do you know any one who wishes, on certain terms, a Paymastership in the E. Indies ?*

" I will enquire about the *other* matters.

" Your's truly,

" R. M."

No. 6.

" Dear Madam,

" I shall ascertain to-morrow every thing respecting the P.ship.

" Will any person you know *like a place in the Bank*, about one hundred pounds per ann.?

"I believe *another* P. ship of a first, and one of a 2d battal. may be had, and militia adjutancies.

"Dear ~~Madam~~,

"Your's truly,

"R. M."

"*Wednesday Aft. Dec. 7.*"

—————

No. 7.

"Dear Madam,   *Thursday, 5 Aft.*

"I have been in search of Mr. Barber, both in Bream's-buildings and the city, without success: I shall see ~~him to-morrow~~ at eleven, and I am *satisfied* ~~I shall~~ arrange with him (I hope as he wishes.)

"In the *mean time*, as it is *certain* Mr. Williams may have what he wishes. I beg you will be so good as to send to Mr. Browne *instantly* to call on ~~me, as it cannot be kept~~ longer than a *day open*; and I think I can satisfy Mr. B. that there will be *no disappointment*. Pray send to him *directly*,

"Your's very truly,

"R. M."

" The receipts to be taken in the short form, as it
is likely Coutts & Co. will not like to sign such a
special receipt as that written by Mr. B.

" 680l. to be deposited at Messrs. Coutts & Co.
            in names of L. & B.
" & 157l. 10s. at Messrs. Birch and Co. in the
            names of —— Blake and Wm. Barber—
" & to take a *similar* receipt."

" It is *absolutely* necessary to make the *deposit* to-
morrow, *Friday*, (if *not already done*) as the appointment otherwise will probably *fail*."

Addressed :

" Mrs. Clarke, Tavistock-Place,
    14, Russel-Square."

———

(*The three following papers are written in pencil.*)

" Forms of Receipt."

" Received   Sept. 1808, of M. Blake and
        the sum of three hundred and sixty-seven
pounds ten shillings, to be repaid by us to the bearer

of this receipt, upon producing the same, indorsed by the said M. Blake and

" (Signed)   BIRCH & Co."

" I do hereby agree to indorse a certain receipt, dated   Sept. 1808, for 367l. 10s. received of M. Blake and myself, by Messrs. Birch, Chambers and Co. immediately on the appointment of

as a clerk on the establishment in the War-office.

" Witness my hand, this   day of Sept. 1808.

" N. B. A similar engagement to be signed as to 52l. 10."

" Received   Sept. 1808, of   and R. Maltby, the sum of fifty two pounds ten shillings, to be repaid by us to the bearer of this receipt, upon producing the same indorsed by the said

and R. Maltby.

" (Signed)   BIRCH & Co."

" Dear Madam,

" It is impossible for me to pay the cash in this day, or even to-morrow, as it is in the Bank. Understanding from you that it would not be wanted for a fortnight, I hope the business will not be stopped for the want of this, for you may rest assured, honour is the order of the day in this transaction, and L. will come up directly and supply the cash. I have made a little alteration in the blank receipt and agreement you sent me, but which I dare say will not be objected to by Lloyd & Co.

" Your's very oby.

" Tuesday. Wm. BARBER."

" Recd. Sept. 1808, of Lloyd, Esq. and William Barber, the sum of to be repaid by us to the bearer of this receipt, upon producing the same indorsed by the said Lloyd and Wm. Barber, or by the said Wm. Barber only, in case such receipt, with the said joint indorsement thereon, shall not be produced to us within two months from the date hereof.

" Signed) COUTTS & Co."

" Agreement.

" I Wm. Barber do hereby agree to indorse a certain receipt, dated Sept. 1808, for

received of John Lloyd, Esq. and myself, by Messrs.
Coutts & Co. immediately on the appointment of
J. K. Lodwick, Esq. to the place of assistant com-
missary, appearing in the London Gazette, provided
such appointment takes place within two months
from the date hereof.   And I, the said John Lloyd,
do hereby agree, that in case the above-mentioned
appointment shall not appear in the London Gazette
within the time above-mentioned, then that I the
said J. Lloyd will indorse over such receipt to the
said Wm. Barber, to enable him to receive such
above mentioned sum from Messrs. Coutt and Co.
so deposited in their hands.

                    " LLOYD.
                    " B."

BARONESS NOLEKIN & MAJOR SHAW'S
LETTERS.

We shall conclude our selection from the written
documents with two letters from the Baroness
Nolekin, who had applied to Mrs. Clarke for a
pension of 400l. per annum. And a letter of com-
plaint from Major Shaw, Barrack-Master at the
Cape of Good Hope, who had been under half-
pay under the following circumstances :

Mrs. Clarke had obtained for him the above situation, for which she had received 500l. with which she not being satisfied, complained to H. R. H. who said " he had told her all along that she had a very bad sort of man to deal with, and that she ought to have been more careful, and that *he would immediately* put him on half pay."

———

No. 1.

" Dear Madam,

" I see by the papers, that the D···· was with the King yesterday morning, and that Mr. Pitt had a private audience of his Majesty, I therefore indulge a hope that my request may have been thought of; do then, my dear Madam, inform me in what state of forwardness it now stands, when and by whom my letter was given, and how received. Pardon my giving you the trouble of answering me *all* these questions, but the very *kind* part you have taken in this business assures me you will pardon me, and think it but natural I should feel *anxious* in a matter of so much consequence to me and mine.   A thousand thanks for the carp you were so good as to send me yesterday, and with my kindest wishes, be assured,

"My dear Madam,

"I remain most sincerely,

"Your most obliged,

"M. NOLEKEN."

"*Thursday, Five o'clock,*

"Mrs. Clarke, 18."

No. 2;

"*Glo'cester-Place, Sept. 22.*

"My dear Madam,

"I am this moment favoured with your very kind letter; this fresh mark of your friendship gives me great pleasure.   I hope the change of air has perfectly restored your health, and that I shall have the satisfaction of seeing you return to town in as good looks as ever.   My dear Baron, with his best respects to you, begs you will have the goodness to assure H. R. H. of the deep sense of gratitude he feels for the Duke's gracious remembrance of him, and thinks

with you that His Mty. would be more liberal to
him than Mr. ———— if he dare presume to judge
from His Mty's goodness to him for these forty years
past, on every occasion. I hope the weather has
been as fine at Margate as in London ; it has, thank
God, quite restored my health.   I flatter myself you
will favour me with a visit on Wednesday, any
time most agreeable to you to name; for, be assured I enjoy very sincerely the pleasure of your
society, exclusive of the gratitude I shall ever feel
for the kind interest you take for me and mine.
Adieu, my dear Madam.

> " Believe me your's most truly,
>
> " M. NOLEKEN.

" Mrs. Clarke, Royal Hotel,
    Margate, Kent."

MAJOR SHAW'S LETTER.

Off Lizard and a fair wind.

" Although I have troubled you so often, and
although my mind is nearly convinced that the
hardships of which I complained HAS been rectified,

3

by the order of *the Gazette in respect to my reduction* being *rescinded*, yet whilst even the suspicion of so serious an evil and indeed an injustice continues, I know that you will make every allowance, and pardon my being so importunate. In addition to the custom of the army being in my favour (as you mentioned), the following instances are specifically so, and in the same appointment: Lieut. Col. Carey, D. B. M. G. Major 28th regt. Lt. Col. Vesey, D. B. M. G. Canada, Lt. Col. 29th regt. the late Colonel Brinsley, D. B. M. G. West Indies, retained also his full pay-commission until his death; and I believe I stand *singular* in the army, in an officer being appointed to the Staff abroad, and reduced on half-pay in consequence. Thus my case bears in point of right. Your feelings will justify my expectations in point of promise and assurances. The first impression of receiving injury at the hands from whence I had trusted to have merited the contrary, are the only excuses I can plead for any intemperance that may have appeared in my letters, you will, I am sensible, as my mind was at the time affected, readily pardon. The period may arrive in which you will know that, independent of particular consideration, I merited your *good offices*; but until circumstances develope themselves, you shall never understand them through me or by my means. However severely I have felt, however warmly I may have expressed myself, of this be assured, that you shall not experience uneasiness of my occasioning. Tho' thus decided at present, yet permit me to say, that it does not arise from *viewing otherwise* the severe and cruel injury of putting me on half-pay. Independent of present mortification, my prospects in the active line of my profession are ruined by it, and, God knows, they are not very brilliant, considering either the length or the nature of my services. Further, Madam, in my present *separation* from *my children*, it creates in me sensations particularly painful, when I reflect, that if approaching that state to which we must all at some period arrive, that I could not (by this measure) have the consolation of resigning my commission *by sale* for the benefit of my *large family*; and that they should in this event have no other *memento* of my *having served 23 years*, than in the ex-

H

pences of the purchase, &c. &c. of some commissions. In such cases the humane consideration of the present Commander in Chief have been eminently distinguished.

" I shall no longer trespass; my only apology rests in that every feeling is involved in the present object. I had even appropriated my full pay for the education of two children remaining in England; but illness has for some time deprived me of all my family. Let me, Madam, owe good offices to you, and I shall be ever grateful. From your explaining this case, I am certain that *his justice* will be extended to me. Let me not be driven from my profession. Do away the present bar to my family joining me at the Cape; for I am sure that your sentiments will accord, that I ought not to serve when no longer with honour and on a *reciprocal* footing with those *similarly appointed.*

" We are not likely, I fear, to be a healthy fleet; some ships are very crowded, and sickness has already made its appearance; and there are two ships,

I hear, without either doctor or medicines. Fare-
wel: and I hope to receive your commands.

" Do away the present evil, and unite the appointments I mentioned, and I will annually remit
300l. Whilst I remain, *remember* do *me justice*, let
not any thing prevent this; allow not self or family
have ever to say, that we owed misfortune to such a
hand."
" Addressed: Mrs. Clarke,
    " Gloucester-place,
" 18.   Portman-square."

AUTHENTIC PARTICULARS

RELATING TO

THE SEPARATION

OF

HIS ROYAL HIGHNESS THE DUKE OF YORK

FROM

MRS. CLARKE.

———

The Public must naturally feel a curiosity, to know what the circumstances were, which led to the separation of his Royal Highness the Duke of York from the subject of these memoirs.

Let us, in the first place, listen to the account given by William Adam, Esq. who, on the first night of this important investigation, rose immediately after Mrs. Clarke had withdrawn, and gave the following statement:

In the year 1789, Mr. Adam was desired by his Royal Highness the Duke of York to look into

some concerns of his, and from that time up to
the present period, he has continued his attention
to those concerns, as he says, not in a *professional*
but *perfectly gratuitous,* and without any emolu-
ment. It came to this gentleman's knowledge,
in the year 1805, that the husband of Mrs. Clarke
threatened an action for crim. con. against the
Duke of York. Mr. Adam was commissioned to
institute an enquiry on this subject; in the
course of which he discovered, that the conduct
of Mrs. Clarke was not so correct as it ought to
have been, and that it had a tendency to prejudice his Royal Highness's interests, not in a military or public point of view, but *his interest, and
his name, with regard to money.* The Royal Duke
was unwilling to believe that there was any thing
improper in the conduct of his mistress, till a certain fact brought these transactions more directly
home to his Royal Highness's attention.

Mr. Adam now directed the enquiry more at
large, and employed Mr. Lowton, an eminent solicitor, who employed Mr. Wilkinson, his *man of*

H 3.

trust, to look into the business ; and early in May, 1806, the result of their investigation was submitted in writing to the Commander in Chief.

Mr. Adam felt he had an unpleasant duty to discharge ; but he was determined that nothing should prevent him from following up the business, and extricating the Royal Duke from the person with whom he was connected.

By direction of his Royal Highness, Mr. Adam had an interview with Mrs. Clarke, during which he conducted the conversation to those points, which led him to discover, with perfect accuracy, how far there was truth or falsehood, in the information which he had obtained in the manner before stated.

It had been represented to Mr. A. that Mrs. Clarke had defended an action as a married woman, having obtained the property for which the action was brought, in the character of a widow.

Investigation was made with regard to the place of her marriage: and it was found she was married a minor at Pancras. She had represented at different times, that her mother was of a family of the name of Mackenzie; that her father was named Farquhar, that they lived in the neighbourhood of Berkhampstead, and that accounts would be had of the family there.

The Berkhampstead Register had been examined with that view for forty years back. In the course of conversation, upon Mr. Adams's interview with Mrs. Clarke, he took occasion to ask her where she was married, when she stated to him seriously and distinctly, that she was married at Berkhampstead. She likewise stated, that her husband was a nephew of Mr. Alderman Clarke, now the chamberlain of London; which was also found, upon investigation, to be untrue.

In a few days after this, his Royal Highness's mind being made up to separate himself from

Mrs. Clarke, Mr. Adam was employed to make a personal communication to her of his Royal Highness's determination. This commission Mr. Adam executed; and accompanied it with a declaration, that the Duke of York thought it his duty, if her conduct was correct, to give her an annuity of 400l. a year, to be paid quarterly; that he could enter into no obligation in writing, by bond or otherwise; that it must rest entirely *upon his word*, (what pity 'twas not *his honour*) to be performed according to her behaviour; and that he might therefore have it in his power to withdraw the annuity in case her behaviour was such as to make him consider that it was unfit it should be paid.

Mrs. Clarke appeared much *surprised*, but by no means *exasperated* at this communication; but she declared her determination to see the Duke again, nay, gave Mr. Adam to understand, that she did not despair of being able to prevail upon him to receive her again under his protection. Indeed, from the billet doux which have found their way to the public, it is not to be wondered, that she should feel very confident of her influence over that royal personage.

Mr. Adam has laboured much to convince the House of Commons, that the investigation into the conduct of Mrs. Clarke, had not for its object any thing connected with her *military transactions;* but merely how far the Duke of York's *name* was likely to be committed by her mode of raising money.

It appears very strange after this, that Mr. Lowton, the gentleman employed in this investigation, should have declared, that he *did not* in any of the enquiries he had made, discover that she *had made use of the Duke of York's name* to raise money ; only it appeared to him, that in consequence of the protection she had from the Duke of York, and the way she lived, many persons were induced to trust her further than he thinks they would have done, if it had not been for that protection. The same gentleman states, that *his enquiries* were of a nature which regarded

Mrs. Clarke's husband and her family, rather than the mode in which she acquired money.

Here is certainly a flat contradiction in evidence: Mr. Adam says, that in the course of his enquiries, he discovered that Mrs. Clarke's conduct had a tendency to injure the Duke's *interests and his name with regard to money.* What can be understood by this, but that Mrs. Clarke employed the name of his Royal Highness for the purpose of raising money ; yet Mr. Lowton, who was employed to conduct the enquiry *more at large,* and reduce it to body and shape, declares, that in the course of this *enlarged enquiry,* he *did not discover* any instance of such conduct in the subject of these memoirs.

But, forsooth, in consequence of the protection she had from the Duke of York, many persons were induced to trust her further than they would have done, if it had not been for that protection. Why surely, it required no investigation to discover this. Mrs. Clarke, like the moon, (asking pardon of Madam Diana for the comparison) derived all the lustre she possessed in Gloucester Place from the *sun* of royalty. This his Royal Highness must have been aware of from the very first; and to represent it as a discovery consequent upon an important investigation, or a motive for the Duke of York's withdrawing his protection from his favorite mistress, is absurd in the extreme.

Mr. Adam deserves every credit for the exertions he has made to save the character of the late illustrious Commander in Chief, particularly as his exertions have been *perfectly gratuitous*, but he should not have made this unfounded attack upon the character of a female no longer under the protecting shield of royalty—thrown at large upon the wide ocean of life, and exposed to all the rude attacks of a merciless world.

Nor does this threat said to have been made by Mrs. Clarke's husband, appear by any means to be a sufficient reason for his Royal Highness's deserting the object of his warm affections.

What had his Royal Highness to dread from the consequences of such a threat ? exposure ? No ; surely his living with Mrs. Clarke was already a matter of sufficient notoriety ; nor can his Royal Highness have been very solicitous about concealing it, having placed her upon a magnificent establishment in Gloucester Place, and knowing, as he must, that it was only through the countenance she received from him, that she could be enabled to support such an establishment.

As to any serious result that could arise from an action of crim. con. under such circumstances, the idea is too absurd to be entertained for a moment ; or even admitting that any thing was to be feared from such a result, it could not be warded off by his leaving her, nor rendered more alarming by his continuing the connection.

Perhaps the torch of love, which blazed so

fiercely at one period, may by this time have nearly burnt out; but this does not appear to have been the case, for several months elapsed, during the progress of this investigation, during which time no alteration appeared in his Royal Highness's conduct to Mrs, Clarke; and the separation seems to have been forced upon him by some strong necessity.

What this necessity was, is now the only point that remains to be settled ; we, for our own part, do not find that any strong case has been made out, if the discovery of Mrs, Clarke's military transactions be not admitted.

Of what does Mr. Adam accuse Mrs. Clarke? What in the course of his elaborate investigation has he discovered that can affect her character? Why, forsooth, the naughty woman told fibs—she said she was married at Berkhampstead, instead of St. Pancras—she said her husband was related to Mr. Alderman Clarke, when he was no more than

the son of a man of property and respectability,—
this is all.

No, No, Mr. Adam, this will not do;—there
must have been some other more substantial
ground for this separation, which appears so hos-
tile to the Royal Duke's feelings; only your having said the contrary, only the deference that must
be paid to your unimpeached honor, can induce
the British nation to believe, that the true result
of your investigation was not the growing notoriety of Mrs. Clarke's military transactions, which
were likely to affect the character of his Royal
Highness in so serious a manner.

The following notes will serve to illustrate how
far it was an extinction of passion that led to the
separation.

No. 1.

" I do not know what you mean; I have
never authorised any body to plague or disturb

you, and therefore you may be perfectly at your ease on my account."

=====

No. 2.

" Inclosed I send you the money which you wished to have for your journey.

" Inclosed, *my Darling* receives the note as well as the money, which she should have had some days ago.

" *My Darling* shall have the ticket for the box the moment I go home.

God bless you."

=====

These notes were addressed to George Farquhar, Esq.

These notes were written subsequent to the separation—the latter when the Duke transmitted

200l. for her journey. Mr. Adam, she says, thought *one hundred* enough.

From hence it appears, that after all the exertions of the disinterested Mr. Adam, the intelligent Mr. Greenwood, and the minutely official Colonel Gordon; after all the minute enquiries by Messrs. Lowton and Wilkinson; after having spent nearly twelve months in lingering deliberation, before the Duke could screw his courage to the sticking place, and copy the dreadful letter of Greenwood, which was a substitute for the appearance of his Royal Highness to dinner in Gloucester Place, the cause of love shielded his votary against this mighty phalanx, consisting of Adam, Greenwood, Gordon, Lowton, and a whole host of the Duke's special *attachees*, who possibly might be jealous of the superior attractions of love to those of interest and the mere formalities of office,—these therefore were the Mentors who pushed the Telemachus from the rock.

We have seen, that as in all the greater departments of church and state, this lady had an interest; thus, in smaller matters, she had so completely dubbed herself directress, and secured the very soul of her Cæsar, that her taste was consulted upon the beauty of a puppy, and the character of a solicitor.

We shall here subjoin the other letters of his Royal Highness to Mrs. Clarke, after separation, that have transpired.

[The following letters were read :]

No. 1.

" Without being informed to what amount you " may wish for assistance, it is impossible for me " to say how far it is in my power to be of use to " you.

 " Friday Morning."
 Addressed:
" Mrs. Clarke,
 " No. 9, Old Burlington-street."

No. 2.

" If it could be of the least advantage to either
" of us, I should not hesitate in complying with
" your wish to see me; but as a meeting must, I
" should think, be painful to both of us, under
" the present circumstances, I must decline it."

    Addressed :
" Mrs. Clarke,
" No. 18, Gloucester-place,
    " Portman-square."

No. 3.

        " October, 21, 1806.

" It is totally out of my power to be able to
" give you the assistance which you seem to ex-
" pect.

    " October 21, 1806.   S.E.
                        A 24
                        806

    Addressed :
" Mrs. Clarke, Southampton.
    " 1 | 4

No. 4.

" I enter fully into your sentiments concerning
" your children, but cannot undertake what I am
" not sure of performing.

" With regard to Weybridge, I think that you
" had better remove your furniture, and then *di-*
" *rect the person who was employed to take the House,*
" *to give it up again.*

Addressed :

" Mrs. Clarke,
" No. 18, Gloucester-place,
" Portman-square."

The following was the annunciation of the
Duke's determination, consequent upon Lowton's
investigation, sent to Mrs. Clarke in the hand
writing of Mr. Greenwood.

[The letter was read.]

" You must recollect the occasion which obli-

" ged me, above seven months ago, to employ
" my Solicitor in a suit with which I was then
" threatened on your account; the result of those
" enquiries first gave me reason to form an unfa-
" vorable opinion of your conduct; you cannot
" therefore accuse me of rashly or hastily decid-
" ing against you: but after the proofs which
" have at last been brought forward to me, and
" which it is impossible for you to controvert, I
" owe it to my own character and situation to
" abide by the resolution which I have taken,
" and from which it is impossible for me to re-
" cede. An interview between us must be a pain-
" ful task to both, and can be of no possible ad-
" vantage to you; I therefore must decline it.
    " May, 1806."

" Copy of a note supposed to have been written
            by the D——."

━━━━━━

The following is a satement made by Colonel
M:Mahon in the House of Commons, relative to

Mrs. Clarke's conduct subsequent to the separation—with Mrs. Clarke's answer.

JOHN M'MAHON, Esq. a Member of the House, attending at his place, made the following Statement.

To my extreme astonishment, I found my name alluded to by the Lady who has just been examined at the Bar; I cannot tell for what possible purpose she has alluded to me; I have nothing to offer to this committee, that has the least relevance, or can throw the smallest light upon any subject whatever, that the Honourable Gentleman has brought before the consideration of this House. In consequence of an anonymous note that was written to His Royal Highness the Prince of Wales, promising very important communications, I did, at the command of the Prince, lightly as he treated the note, nevertheless call at No. 14, Bedford-row, Russell-square, where the note was dated from. Upon going there, the woman who opened the door, and from whom I.

thought I saw much that told me she had put that note into the penny-post or the twopenny post herself, I asked her the name of the lady of the house, that I wanted to see; she desired me to tell my name; I told her I could give her no name, but produced the note, which she immediately remembered to have put into the twopenny post, and said it was written by her Mistress. I was then conducted into the house, into a parlour, where certainly there were a great many of those morocco concerns, which she has mentioned before, for there were ten chairs I think set round the table, from the supper or the dinner of the day before; after remaining some time, I was conducted up stairs, where I saw the lady, whose name I was told to be Farquhar. The lady in perfect good humour came out and received me; and I held the note I was possessed with, as my credentials, for her communicating whatever she might think fit to tell a third person, not pressing her to any communication which she ought not to give to me. She told me, that she would communicate nothing to a third person; I then told her that it was impossible that I could hold up any expectation of an interview with such a person as the one to whom the letter was addressed, unless she gave me some clue, or some plausible pretence for it, and that I had no idle curiosity to gratify. She then entered into a conversation of so general and so extraordinary a nature, that I am confident this House would not for one moment entertain it, because the tendency and intention of it was to make bad blood between two illustrious Brothers, whose affections could never be shaken by any such representation, at least I am confident that the illustrious person I have the pride and glory to serve and love, would be incapable. She then told me she would shew me letters to prove and to establish, that there was a hatred on one part to the other; I declined seeing any letters; she then said, I would commit those letters to you, for the persusal of the illustrious Personage; to which I, as my bounden duty and firm conviction, said, if they were lying at his feet, he would scorn to look at one of them. In this interview, at first, I stated that I thought she was

a friend of Mrs. Clarke; she said, Certainly she
knew Mrs. Clarke extremely intimately, that
there was nobody she loved and regarded as she
did Mrs. Clarke; that she perfectly knew her.
She then asked me if I knew Mrs. Clarke; I said
I do not. "Do you know her, Sir, by person?"
I said, I believed not. "Do you know her by
character;" Yes, said I, her fame is very cele-
brated; and I have heard of Mrs. Clarke, but
know nothing of her myself. She asked me then
what I knew; I said, it certainly was not to her
advantage; but I had heard the Duke of York
had been very generous to her, and that she had
not been very grateful on her part; but that was
only from information I had received. She then
proceeded to state, what I throw myself on the
consideration of the House, as it might be the effect of passion, and appeared to me a disposition
to gratify her revenge by representations that I
do not think the House would for a moment permit me to expose, when it went to a tendency to
make bad blood between two Brothers. We then
proceeded. I soon after said, "I am speaking to

Mrs. Clarke herself:" I thought so, from several
things she told me, that I wish not to repeat; I
said, " I am confident I am addressing myself to
Mrs. Clarke herself;" She laughed, and said,
" I am Mrs. Clarke." I then begged her a thousand pardons for the portrait I had drawn, but
disclaimed being the painter. " I am sure you
are not, for it was Adam and Greenwood that
gave you my character." We then proceeded,
till she made a statement, that I have no hesitation in declaring to this Committee did, in its
statement, appear such as I could with honour
and character entertain and listen to ; that, under every compassionate feeling and sentiment, I
felt no indisposition to listen to and entertain.
She stated to me, that Mr. Adam had called upon
her, and in a very firm, but steady manner, told
her, that the Duke of York was determined to
separate from her; but that if she retired into
the country, and conducted herself with propriety
and decorum, he would allow her 400l. a year;
that she had accordingly so retired into Devonshire
for several months, but failing to receive the re-

I

mittances she expected, she had been driven to
town for the purpose of gaining her arrear, and
placing her annuity upon a more regular mode
of payment; that if that condition was complied
with, by the payment of her arrear, and of secu-
ring the punctuality of it to her in future, his
Royal Highness should never hear any more
about her.   Upon the fairness of this statement,
supposing it to be true, (I do not pretend to say
what my opinion of it was) I said, if your statement, Mrs. Clarke, is correct and orthodox, I will
certainly wait upon Mr. Adam, and state it to
him, to know where the objection lies to the payment of your annuity.   That was in the month of
July last.   Mr. Adam had gone, two days after I
saw Mrs. Clarke, into Scotland, and had not returned when I came back to London in October,
therefore I never saw him, but at the persuasion
of Mrs. Clarke, by a letter she wrote to me, she
saying that his Royal Highness was prepared to
hear what I had to say, as she had told it to him.
I had the honour of waiting upon the Duke of
York, and telling his Royal Highness exactly

what she had stated, not pretending to vouch for its veracity in any shape whatever. His Royal Highness's immediate and prompt answer to me was, her conduct is so abominable, that I will hear nothing at all about her. Any thing I could possibly offer after what I have now said would be superfluous; there is the conclusion, that is the epilogue of any thing I have to state; and as to any question thought proper by the honourable gentleman, or any circumstances he has cited or remarked upon, I am as ignorant as a man unborn.

The following is an extract from Mrs. Clarke's examination, with the notes of Colonel M'Mahon, which Mrs. Clarke laid before the House agreebly to her promise.

Do you know Colonel M'Mahon ?—Yes.

Did you ever write an anonymous letter to his Royal Highness the Prince of Wales ?—I wrote a few lines to his Royal Highness the Prince of

Wales, stating that a person wished to see him, and Colonel M'Mahon called.

Did you sign your own name, at any name, to those few lines which you sent to the Prince of Wales?—It was only a few lines without any name, and Colonel M'Mahon called in consequence, and when the servant opened the door, he asked, who kept the house; Mrs. Farquhar, that was my mother. When he came up stairs into the drawing room, he said, Mrs. Farquhar, how do you do; what is the business; I told him, that I wished to see the Prince of Wales, and after a few minutes conversation, Colonel M'Mahon found that I was Mrs. Clarke; he then promised to communicate the message to the Prince, and the next day brought me a very civil message from his Royal Highness, stating that he was extremely sorry he was obliged to go out of town to Brighton, which he did do that morning, that it was impossible for him to interfere, that he had a very great respect for me, was sorry for the manner in which I had been treated, and that Colonel M'Mahon might use his influence with the Duke of York to be the bearer of any message that might be the means of making peace ; but that it was a very delicate matter for his Royal Highness to interfere with his brother. Several notes passed between Colonel M'Mahon and me, and several interviews. He mentioned to me, that he had seen his Royal Highness the Duke of York at one time, I think in July, that the Duke of York asked him, if I was not very much exasperated against him, and if I did not use very strong language, and abuse him. Colonel M'Mahon said, quite the contrary, Sir, I assure you ; Mrs. Clarke is very mild towards you, and she lays the whole of the blame on Mr. Adam ; he said, she is very right, I will see into her affairs. That was the end of the first message. I think the last message that Colonel M'Mahon brought me was, that he could not bring his Royal Highness to any terms at all, to any sort of meaning concerning the debts, and although I had behaved so very handsome towards his Royal Highness, and had exacted nothing but his own promises to be put in execution, or even to take the sum that was due to me upon the annuity and pay the trades-

men, and then I would let his Royal Highness off
of the debts, as that perhaps would satisfy them;
that he considered it as very fair, and very honourable, and very liberal, or he would not have
been the bearer of those messages; and he said,
he esteemed me very much, from the character I
bore among my female acquaintances that he was
intimate with, I mean women of character, and
for the services I had done to many poor young
men within his knowledge.

I will bring some of his notes, or give them to
Colonel Wardle, to be read here to-morrow, to
corroborate what I have stated.

"*Monday Morning.*

"Colonel M'Mahon presents his best compli-
"ments to Mrs. Clarke, and had only yesterday
"the pleasure to receive her note of Thursday
"last, for although he has returned to town for
"the season, as his head-quarters, he makes two
"or three days excursions from it as often as he
"can, and it was during one of those that Mrs.
"Clarke's note arrived, otherwise it should not

" have so long remained unanswered.   Col. M.
" will take the first forenoon he possibly can to
" wait on Mrs. Clarke in the course of this
" week"

Addressed :

" Mrs. Clarke,
" No. 14, Bedford-Place, Bloomsbury."

———

(Private)   " *Wednesday Morning.*

" I should be most happy to bring about your
" wishes, and render you any service with the
" D. of Y. but I have not been able to see him
" since I had the pleasure of seeing you; and I
" understand he goes to Windsor to-day and
" stays till Friday, when I will try all in my
" power to seek an audience on your business,
" but am obliged to go out of town myself until
" that day. A thousand thanks for the loan of
" your seal, from which I have had an impression
" taken, in remembrance of your sprightly device.

" Ever your's

" Mrs. Farquhar,   J. M.
" 14, Bedford-Place, Russel-square."

We have now arrived at the conclusion of our important task. We have presented our readers with a faithful narrative of the life of Mrs. Clarke, from the best authorities we have been able to collect.

We have, with the impartial hand of truth, gone through that body of evidence which the late important enquiry has produced : we have not touched lightly on the subject : we have given it pretty much at large, for it is that alone which has given celebrity to our heroine, and had it never been produced, public curiosity would never have called upon us for the production of these memoirs.

. We declared, at the outset of the present work, that we had no intention to pronounce judgement upon the question at issue between his Royal Highness the Duke of York and the British public ; nor have we done so,—but we feel it a duty incumbent upon us to offer our candid opinion upon the whole matter, which we here offer for our reader's inspection.

We leave, in a great measure, to such of our Bishops and churchmen, who prefer the interests of religion and morality to the mammon of this world, and such we undoubtedly have, to enlarge upon the vices of the illustrious personage, now so much the object of general conversation, and to point out the baneful influence of pernicious example so exalted, upon public morals and public decency. This is not our province. A character like his Royall Highness the Duke of York, born in the lap of luxury, of wealth, and profusion, surrounded from his birth by those who are too apt to administer any thing rather than the wholesome draught of good counsel, who are too prone to flatter and encourage those passions which they ought to check, and, if possible, to smother; such a character is necessarily surrounded by many temptatations.

We are impressed with a conviction, that fidelity to the marriage contract is the chief bond that holds society together. In proportion as this sacred tie is trampled upon, we degenerate towards a state of primitive rudeness and barbarity. But whilst we contend for the inviolability of the conjugal engagement, we contend also that the knot of Hymen should never be tied but by the hands of love.

Alas! who can say that this is the case in the present generation, who takes but a casual survey of public manners. Interest is the idol to which every affection of the heart is sacrificed. Parents, in the exercise of that control which they necessarily must have over the conduct of their children, think not of what is most agreeable to their dispositions so much as what they themselves deem most eligible.

If any are entitled to our pity in this respect more than others, they must be the sons and daughters of Royalty. Forbidden to marry out of a certain rank, political interests, or the will of a beloved parent may often induce them to form a nuptial engagement in which the heart has no share. Nature, who will not suffer her power to be insulted by human authority, never fails, on some occasions, to exert her sway, and to awaken those latent sympathies which lie hidden in the secret.

Her diamonds were in pawn for 800l. with Birkett's, and she released them out of the money which Mr. Dowler gave her for his appointments.

Mr. Percival has stated, by authority of the Duke of York, that during her residence in Gloucester-Place, his Royal Highness, in different ways, expended fifteen thousand pounds upon Mrs. Clarke; but even admitting this statement to be correct, how could this sum be sufficient during a period of three years, to support an establishment, which Lord Folkstone has declared he could not maintain under 10,000l. per annum.

For the last three months of her living with the Duke, he never advanced her a single farthing; she was under *three thousand pounds* in debt when the establishment in Gloucester-Place broke up; the Duke of York, we must add, from the testimony of Mrs. Clarke, gave her 500l. when she first went to Gloucester-Place, which was laid out in linen and other articles, and previous to dissolving the connection, he gave her the lease of the house; but upon the sale of this, when she had paid 700l. to the servants, and the poorer tradesmen, and Mr. Harry Phillips had deducted 4 or 500l. for his commission, there was no balance coming to her.

Admitting these facts, who can accuse Mrs. Clarke of selfishness or rapacity.

The grand question now presents itself—how did Mrs. Clarke support the establishment in Gloucester-Place? When asked by the committee of the House of Commons how she obtained the money for that purpose, she answers, with great *naivete*, " Some of the money has come before the House, and *the manner in which I used to get it;*" and upon being questioned as to how soon she began these practices, she replies, "I never began it till I felt distressed, and the hints I had from his Royal Highness; *he told me that I had always more interest than the Queen had, and that I might use it."*

It has been said, that 999 out of every thousand individuals in the British nation, would be found of opinion that his Royal Highness the Duke of York is guilty of the charges that have been brought against him by Mr. Wardle. We must own that the result of those popular meetings, which have hitherto taken place on the subject, go very much in confirmation of this assertion.

When Mr. Wardle introduced the subject of the inquiry, much satisfaction was professed by Mr. Canning, Mr. Yorke, Mr. Perceval, and various members, on each side of the house, and much exultation at the anticipated result,—the complete exculpation of the Commander in Chief. Mr. Yorke, in particular, expressed his joy " at seeing the charges brought forward at last in a " *tangible shape.*" These charges have assumed a " tangible shape" with a witness; and what has been proved at the bar, is sufficient to turn the joy of these gentlemen into mourning.

It has been proved—That Mrs. Clarke, kept a most expensive establishment at Gloucester-Place; and that she farther had an establishment at Weybridge, adjoining Oatlands Park, the country residence of the Duke. *It has been proved*—That Mrs. Clarke was in the habit of receiving considerable sums from persons to induce her to procure, by her influence, promotions in the army, and places in different departments under government: in various instances her exertions appear to have been attended with success. *It has been proved*—That applications were made to her respecting church preferments (in the cases of Mr. Beazeley, Mr. Glasse, and Dr. O'Meara). *It has been proved* on the unwilling but unimpeachable evidence of Dr. Thynne, and Mr. Knight, that applications was made to Mrs. Clarke to expedite, by "her supposed influence with his Royal Highness," an exchange for Col. Knight; that the exchange was almost immediately effected, and that Mrs. C. received 200l. for her services. *It has been proved*—That Mrs. C. received a considerable sum for her "suppose influence" in procuring a levy for Col. French. That the Duke was acquainted with some of the particulars respecting this business, appears from the evidence of Miss Taylor, who notwithstanding the severity with which she

has been treated by Mr. Perceval, for a supposed
mistake, which turned out to be his own, " her
character and claims to credit," Mr. W. Smith,
with other members, declared, " were yet unshaken."
—From her evidence it appears, that in a conversation at which the witness was present, in answer to
a question from Mr. C. the Duke replied—" I
am worried with Col. French's levy; *but how*, Darling *does he behave to you?* Mrs. C. answered, But
indifferently, very midling; on which the Duke
said—*Then Col. French had better take care of
himself, or I shall cut up him and his levy too.*" It
has been proved on the evidence of Gen. Clavering,
(who in volunteering his service to impeach the
veracity of Mrs. Clarke, has most completely displayed his own folly) that he applied to her to
obtain leave " to raise a regiment of volunteers out
of the militia, and offered her 1000l. should he
receive his appointment." *It has been proved* in the
case of Mr. Dowler,—That he paid Mrs. C. 1000l.
for her supposed service in procuring him the
valuable place of commissariat. *It has been proved*
from the letters of Mr. Elderton, and several other

persons, who paid Mrs. C, different sums of money,
that they considered her as the instrument by which
their objects were procured.   *It has been proved,—*
That Samuel Carter, Mrs. C's footman, who had
been used to wait at table, stand behind her carriage,
and perform a variety of offices in common with
her other servants, was at the age of 19, elevated to
an ensigncy, and that he is now an officer on the
staff.   Carter's letters to Mrs. Clarke, shew in
grateful language, that he considered himself as
indebted to her for his advancement.

We have purposely omitted noticing any case the
truth of which depends merely on the evidence of
Mrs. Clarke.   She has, indeed, throughout all her
tedious and severe examinations, and crossexami-
nations, persisted in the declaration with which
she set out, that " the Duke was acquainted with
the whole of her transactions respecting the disposal
of commissions."   On her last examinations she
confirmed the account she had before given, respecting her practice of " pinning up at the head of her
bed a list of promotions, and the Duke of York's

drawing up the curtains, taking down the list, reading it over, observing that he would do every one by degrees, putting it in his pocket book, &c." The inconsistencies which have been noticed in Mrs. Clarke's conduct, such as having at times described herself as a widow, assumed false names, &c. are such as might naturally be expected from a person of her manner of life. With respect to the essential parts of her evidence, there certainly have not appeared greater inaccuracies than in the evidence given by some honourable gentlemen, who in the course of the inquiry have found it requisite to *correct* some particulars of their statements previously given. How far the evidence of Mrs. Clarke, in its most important parts, is confirmed by the evidence of others whose characters are unimpeachable, remains for the judgment of the public.

On the close of the examination, which would alone fill a large volume, a motion was made by Mr. Wardle for an address to the King, to dismiss the Duke from his situation of Commander in Chief, and Captain General, was solemnly argued for the unprecedented period of six days, during which, all the eloquence and talents of the country were displayed. The speakers on the side of the people were, Messrs. Wardle, Burdett, Whitbread, Wilberforce, Bankes, Bathurst, Wynne and Smith, and the Lords Folkstone, Milton, Petty, and Temple; and on the side of the Duke, the Chancellor of the Exchequer, the Attorney and Solicitor General, the late and present Secretary of War, the Welsh Judge Burton, Mr. Secretary Canning, and some other members or connections of administration.

Three amendments were moved, by the Chancellor of the Exchequer, by Mr. Bankes, and Mr. Bathurst.

At length there appeared on a division for Mr. Wardle's address, 126 against it.

For the Chancellor of the Exchequer's amendment 278, and against it 196. For Mr. Bankes's amendment 199, and against it 294.

But on the interval, between the adjourned debate on Mr. Bathurst's amendment, the Duke of York RESIGNED HIS OFFICE, and thus was terminated the struggle.

If his Royal Highness had remained in office till the *full extent* of his merits had been discussed, he might, probably, have undergone a rebuke, which would not only have rendered his continuance in office most indecent, but have drawn the public vigilance for ever after towards *those habits which he has given us no pledge, or promise, or even hint of dismissing,* habits which of course as they are the oldest so they must be the dearest habits of his life, and as they are the dearest, *will in all human probability last him all his life.* A man of his long indulgences and his gross want of mind, who, without self-dignity, without studies, without the least elegant resource, loathes the placid enjoyments of his father's fire-side, and flies from prostitute to prostitute for what he calls " the happiness of life," is not likely to give up his pleasures for wisdom he does not understand, and virtues he never practised. If such a man as Johnson was making vows to get up early till he was past seventy and never could accomplish them, if the great Addison took to petty habits of drinking on account of a stupid wife who disregarded him, if Peter the Great could never conquer his fits of anger, in short, if the greatest men, who in their several tracks have shewn such an eager thirst for glory, could not get rid of the little passions that perpetually turned them aside to baser streams, what in the name of reason and experience is to be said for the Duke of York, except that he has none of their wisdom, and therefore as far as his folly goes has a better excuse for his vices? We think Mrs. Clarke had a very good opportunity of understanding his Royal Highness's character, and it was not the least memorable of her observations on him when she said, that were he compelled to live at Oatlands, he would cut his throat. What there is at Oatlands to render it a cave of despair we know not, or how far a prince who lives with his wife has a reasonable ground of suicide; but this we know, that there is an obstinate pride in folly which endears its errors to it the more they are

pointed out, and that a man of weak head, who has
been quaffing one intoxicating draught till he is
forty-five will most likely be drunk all his life. That
his Royal Highness has resigned is certainly an excellent thing, since it gives us at once the end for
which the enquiry was instituted? but this resignation, like all his other acts, should be shewn in its
proper light, since a true knowledge of the *cause*
will be a much greater blessing to the nation than
any effect that has been yet produced.

We shall conclude our observations on this head
in the energetic words of Dr. South, which we
wish were engraved on the heart of every Prince,
and, in short, of every man in a public station.—
" *The wicked, vicious, and scandalous examples of
persons in place and power, are strong temptations to
sin.* For amongst the prime motives of human
actions, next to laws, most reckon examples, and
some place examples above them; for although
there may be a greater authority in laws, yet there
is a greater force, because a greater suitableness, in
examples; and then experience shews, that is not

K

so much what commands, as what agrees, which
gains upon the affections; and the affections, we
all know, are the grand springs and principles of
action. So that if a Prince, for instance, gives
himself up to lewdness and uncleanness, there is
no doubt but whoring will soon come into fashion,
and that he will quickly find more by a great many
to follow him in his lusts, than to obey him in his
laws! If a prince be a breaker of his word,
his oath, or his solemn promise, it may prove
a shrewd temptation to others to do the like by him.
And then he may thank his own example, if he
suffers by the imitation. If a clergyman be noted
for sensuality, covetousnes, or ambition, he may
preach his heart out in behalf of the contrary
virtues, and all to no purpose; for still his example
will be a stronger temptation to the sin, than his
doctrine can be an enforcement of the duty.

" The sins of *Princes* and *Priests* are of a
spreading, and a reigning contagion; and though
naturally they are no more than the acts of particular
persons, yet virtually and consequently, they are

often the sins of a whole community. And if so, good God! What huge heaps of foul guilt must lie at such sinners doors!

" For every person of *note*, *power*, and *place*, living in an open violation of any one of God's laws, holds up a flag of defiance against heaven, and calls in all about him, to fight under his lewd banner against God, and his express commands ; and so, (as it were), by a kind of homage and obedience, to be as vile and wicked as himself ; and when it comes to this, then all the villanies, which were committed by others in the strength and encouragement of his devilish example, will be so personally charged upon his account, and as a just debt exacted of him to the utmost farthing !"

It is not to be supposed, however, that the resignation of the Commander in Chief can possibly put a stop to the spirit of patriotism and inquiry which has gone forth on this occasion. It is not too much to say, that, notwithstanding the present inquiry is closed, all eyes, as it were, remain fixed upon Mrs. Clarke, Mr. Wardle, and his friends; while their enemies have scarcely a single advocate all over the kingdom. The outrages committed upon the publick purse and upon the public feeling, have been too daring to be easily forgotten. Mrs. Mary Anne Clarke, although she has changed her splendid residence in Gloucester-Place, for a more humble dwelling in Westbourne-Place, Chelsea, is still regarded as the original occasion of the good that has already resulted to the public. Much to Mrs. Clarke's credit, she has long supported an aged mother : her children, two girls and a boy, are still living; they have also been provided for by their mother, whose means for continuing this care, will no doubt be increased by the additional eclat which she has acquired.

Colonel Wardle, who has so justly partaken of the public approbation, as a parliamentary men has been hitherto rather obscure. He is a native of Cheshire, and possesses a considerable fortune. During the insurrection in Ireland, he served as

Lieutenant-colonel in the regiment under Sir Watkin Williams Wynne. In fact, he was only returned to Parliament for the Borough of Oakhampton, in 1807. Thus, though a *stripling* in the war of words, yet; excepting Sir Francis Burdett and his few friends, Colonel Wardle has done more towards bringing down the *Goliath* of *Corruption*, than all the rest of the parliamentary phalanx joined together.

He is now, after his labours, enjoying his well-earned feast of applause. The city of Westminster has voted its thanks to him and the minority which supported his motion.

The first corporation in the kingdom have voted the same gentleman their freedom in a gold box, value 100 guineas, and have accompanied their vote with resolutions, declaring that Col. Wardle has proved his charges against the Duke of York, and effected his removal from the important situation he lately held.

K 3

We will not press any further so delicate a subject; but indulge a hope that the late enquiry, painful as it may have been to the feelings of our beloved Sovereign, and to other illustrious individuals, deeply as it must have concerned every British heart, may yet produce the most salutary effects for our country.

The following Letters having been handed about society they have come into our possession, and we here insert them as models of amatory epistles for the sons of rank and fashion.

" My Dear Mary Anne,

" I am engaged this evening to play at whist with *Old Snuffy* : the moment I can escape from the set I will fly to the dear embraces of my beloved darling.

∗∗∗∗∗∗∗   ∗∗∗"

" My Dearest, Dearest, Dear,

" How can I sufficiently express my love to you for your kind note of this morning : expect me by nine, I will fly sooner if there is the least possibility of escaping from the beings I am now with. ∗∗∗∗ shall be attended to because my darling wishes it. Adieu, a long adieu, for eight long hours, and then for the loved embraces of my dearest dear.

∗∗∗   ∗∗∗∗∗"

———

MRS. CLARKE'S MEMOIRS.

So various have been the reports respecting this publication and its suppression, that before we take leave of our readers we present them with the following particulars relative to it, drawn from sources of undoubted authority.

Mrs. Clarke called on Sir Richard Phillips for the purpose of making some arrangement respecting the publication of her Memoirs. Sir Richard Phillips declined to publish the work, for several reasons of a private and political nature; perhaps, not choosing to expose himself to public notice, as the publisher of a work which was likely to create much political interest, at least while the novelty of the thing lasted. The unqualified, and, we trust, unjust reproaches, to which Sir Richard Phillips has of late been exposed, have doubtless taught him some useful lessons of caution and reserve. Though Sir Richard Phillips declined to become the purchaser

of Mrs. Clarke's MS. he promised to recommend
her to a publisher who would treat her justly and li-
berally. At the same time, Sir Richard told Mrs.
Clarke, he conceived, if she could obtain the ar-
rears of her annuity from the Duke, and a legal
settlement for the payment of it in future, together
with the payment of all debts contracted during her
late connection with his Royal Highness, it would
much better answer her purpose to suppress the publication altogether. To this reasonable proposition,
Mrs. Clarke immediately consented. But a difficulty arose as to the means of making this known
to such persons as had it in their power to carry the
plan into execution. Sir Richard accordingly agreed
to open the business to a certain noble Lord, to
whom he made known the projected plan of accommodation. On this a string of propositions
were drawn up, and assented to by Mrs. Clarke;
and the threatened Memoirs of this Lady, written
by herself, was a few days ago consigned to the
flames at Mr. Gillet's, the printer, in Salisbury-
square.

к 5

Eighteen thousand copies, with the perusal of which the country was to have been indulged, have actually been thus destroyed. Mr. Gillett, who was to have published the work, has been paid 1500*l.* and Mrs. Clarke has been most amply indemnified for its suppression, by having *ten thousand pounds* paid down, besides being secured in an annuity of 400*l.* a-year for herself, and 200*l.* a-year for her two daughters; her son is also to be provided for! Besides suppressing these " Memoirs," Mrs. Clarke has given up *Ninety Private Letters,* containing, it is said, anecdotes of " illustrious" and noble personages, of the most curious and even *astonishing* description. So, after all the talk about the *purity* of the age we live *in,* it is thought necessary to buy up at an immense cost these *proofs* of the corruption and profligacy of the higher order of society! What do you say, Mr. Percival, to this? or you, Mr. Adam, who for 20 years have been the *confidential adviser* of the late " illustrious" Commander in Chief? Like the cant of Jacobinism, the cant of " purity" will no longer serve to shield hypocrisy or shelter knavery. Mrs. Clarke has now enough to support herself and family; if she is not wholly lost to decency and decorum, she will retire into privacy; and reflecting upon the folly, the vice, and the misery of her past life, endeavour to atone for it by setting her children the example of a reformed conduct, such as can alone promise either to them or herself security and peace. Mrs. Clarke undoubtedly possesses a considerable portion of good sense; let her now use it in the proper way, let her learn to respect herself and society, and the public, benefited as they must be by the matters brought to light through her means, will think of her in future with feelings of compassion, if not of respect. But if, unmindful of the past and regardless of the future, she still proceeds in her gay career of splendid guilt, she will sink into a vile old age, loaded with contempt, and despised even by those who think " the honour of a Prince" a sufficient cover for impudence and vice.

FREDERICK THE GREAT

AND THE

FAIR MARY ANNE.

AN HISTORICAL BALLAD.

A chieftain of rank to a Cyprian of fame,
  His addresses most fervently paid,
Tho' the altar of Hymen had sanction'd a claim,
And his breast had once glow'd with a legaliz'd flame,
So sacred, so solemn, that no other dame
  His affections should ever have staid.

Tho' the hero was great, he was luckless in arms,
  And oft' from the enemy ran,
By shaking the dice-box he erst lost his farms,
And tho' in one * Venus he met with alarms,
For him there were others had numberless charms,
  And the Bishop was sunk in the man.

* The lucky die was called Venus by the ancients.

In vain did the D—ch—ss her graces display,

   In vain the F—d M—sh—l entreat,

Neither H-rs-e G-d-s, nor O-ds, nor yet levee day,

Nor reviews, nor ridottos, nor races, nor play,

Fix'd his mind, when intent on an object away,

   Whom he ardently nam'd as his sweet.

By his sov'reign tho' rais'd to distinguish'd command

   Unlike young Telemachus' sire,

Voluptuous Pleasure he took by the hand,

And transform'd by the touch of a Circean wand,

He revell'd, and grovell'd, and leagu'd with a band,

   Who had wallow'd in infamy's mire.

Surrounded by Syrens, he never would hear

   The people's admonishing voice,

To remonstrance he gave but the wax-deafen'd ear,

He heeded not counsel, no Mentor was near,

And of Jacobin measures he sure had no fear,

   When a Jacobin* Club was his choice.

       * See Mr. Whitbread's speech.

Integrity spurn'd, and merit disown'd,

   No captains were found on his list,

Who, tho' long in the service, in misery groan'd,

And their direful misfortunes in secret bemoan'd,

   Inferiors to those who were proudly enthron'd,

* On the bed-post which F-d-k kist.

The conjugal tie of affection beside,

   In his letters to fair Mary Anne,

He avows to be slack, and he ne'er will divide

What he feels for his *dear little darling*, with bride,

And tho' (curs'd be his stars) to a wife he is ty'd,

   He will yet be as loose as he can.

Parental respect than a feather or straw,

   It is plain that he valu'd no more,

When he broke thro' that bond which all others will

     awe,

Acknowledg'd a sacred inviolate law.

† But with which *he* diverted the high-season'd maw,

   Of a rav'ning and scandalous w——

---

* See Mrs. Clarke's evidence.

† For which see the title of " snuffy" given to a certain personage.

The patriot Virtues' invincible band
  Thro' disgust and dismay had now fled,
Disquiet and terror now stalk'd o'er the land,
And tho' popular clamour had lighted the brand,
No Briton was found to uplift it in hand,
  And all was but murmur and dread.

At length a bold Cambrian fearlessly came,
  A warrior too as we're told,
Who pok'd from the embers of Jealousy's flame,
Such records as fully establish his fame,
Both reckless of terror, and eke not so tame
  As to barter his glory for gold.

The national council's assembl'd in doubt,
  Of the truths which this champion displays,
Some worms crept in, and some others† crept out,
And they sport on his folly and rashness about,
While poor Clarke in her evidence all of them flout,
  Yet she gives it correct at her ease.

    ♣ Mr. S-rd-n to wit.

Now the minister's muster the blind and the halt,
  Prepar'd to withstand the attack;
But they're told by a patriot factor of malt,
In speeches full fraught with the true attic salt,
That his country with justice would hold him in fault,
  If he drudg'd as a treasury hack.

Sir Francis, the terror of knaves and of fools,
  Is found a true knight in the lists,
Untutor'd in any but Liberty's school,
He knows of no axioms, he knows of no rules,
Such as those which deliver'd by government tools,
  Would envelop the case in their mists.

St. Stephen's attracts now the eyes of the land,
  And it's roofs with long speeches rebound,
When behold the grave Abbot produc'd in his hand,
A Duke's royal honour by P—l plann'd,
But Whitbread oppos'd, and it now only fann'd
  The flame which was playing around.

Amongst other grave *lawyers* who handl'd the case,

   A *hoarse-cawing** raven* is found,

He wants but THREE PARSONS † the minutes to grace,

If the witness such *parsons* could possibly trace,

What a *judge* he will be when he sits in his *place*,

   Upon distant American ground.

Stiff prejudice great one's may humble so low,

   As to give them a place in my rhyme‡,

For we're told that the K—g has aversions to O

As strong as if ask'd to salute the Pope's toe,

Ceremonial which ev'ry true Briton must know,

   Is a vile and a heathenish crime.

* 'Tis said this gentleman croaked to some purpose, at least there is something ominous in his nesting in the largest legal wig of Canada.

† " Still harping on my daughter."   HAMLET.

‡ Vide Dr. O'Meara.

Let not rubicund F-ll-r, howe'er, be forgot,
 Tho' by some he is called a *black dog*,*
And others, again, have yclep'd him a sot,
(With two bottles of port he'll perform what not)
Besides, he professes to tame those who trot
 In barren Hibernian bog.

In vain would the minstrel attempt on the lyre,
 The praises of those who oppos'd,
Fit subjects alone to awaken the fire,
Which dwelt in the numbers of poetry's sire,
With their object attain'd, they have all they desire,
 In beholding corruption depos'd.

The wish of the people at length is obtain'd,
 For an honest minority stood,
Over whom tho' the Ministry 'vantage had gain'd;
Yet the Duke was too wise not to know there re-
 main'd
The reserve of the country, who always maintain'd
 Their liberties bought with their blood.

* See his famous speech on that occasion.

'Tis said, when at sermon ne ever attends,
    And the priest on morality speaks,
He's observ'd as if sitting on sharp needle ends;
He's both troubled himself, and he troubles his
      friends,
So much the immaculate word ever tends
    To suffuse the red glow on his cheeks.

If tradition be true, we are told that he goes
    To attend at the Jewish Passover,
And hopes that some Messiah,† yet under rose,
Will redeem him from trouble, and end all his
      woes;
Then restor'd to command, he will punish his
      foes,
    And again be a prodigal lover.

† Perhaps his locum tenens Sir David.

The red-coated knaves who attempted to bark,

    *From the army he swears he will drum 'em,

And the profits of Osn- -gh given to Clarke,

Are no inconvenience, he swears by the ark;

†The benevolent Jew will supply ev'ry mark,

    And invest him with Urim and Thummum.

* Why was not General Fergusson employed in the late expedition, as he had served with such credit on the same ground before?

† Mr. Goldsmid : to whom I beg leave to say, in the language of the Revelations :—" I have a few things against thee, because thou hast there them who hold the doctrine of Balaam ; who taught Balak to cast a stumbling block before the children of Israel, to eat things sacrificed unto Idols, and to commit fornication." 14th v. c. ji Revel.

FINIS.

Plummer, Printer, Seething-Lane.

Lightning Source UK Ltd.
Milton Keynes UK
UKOW010112220113

205175UK00005B/199/P